TRAVELS IN ARAB COUNTRIES

2007

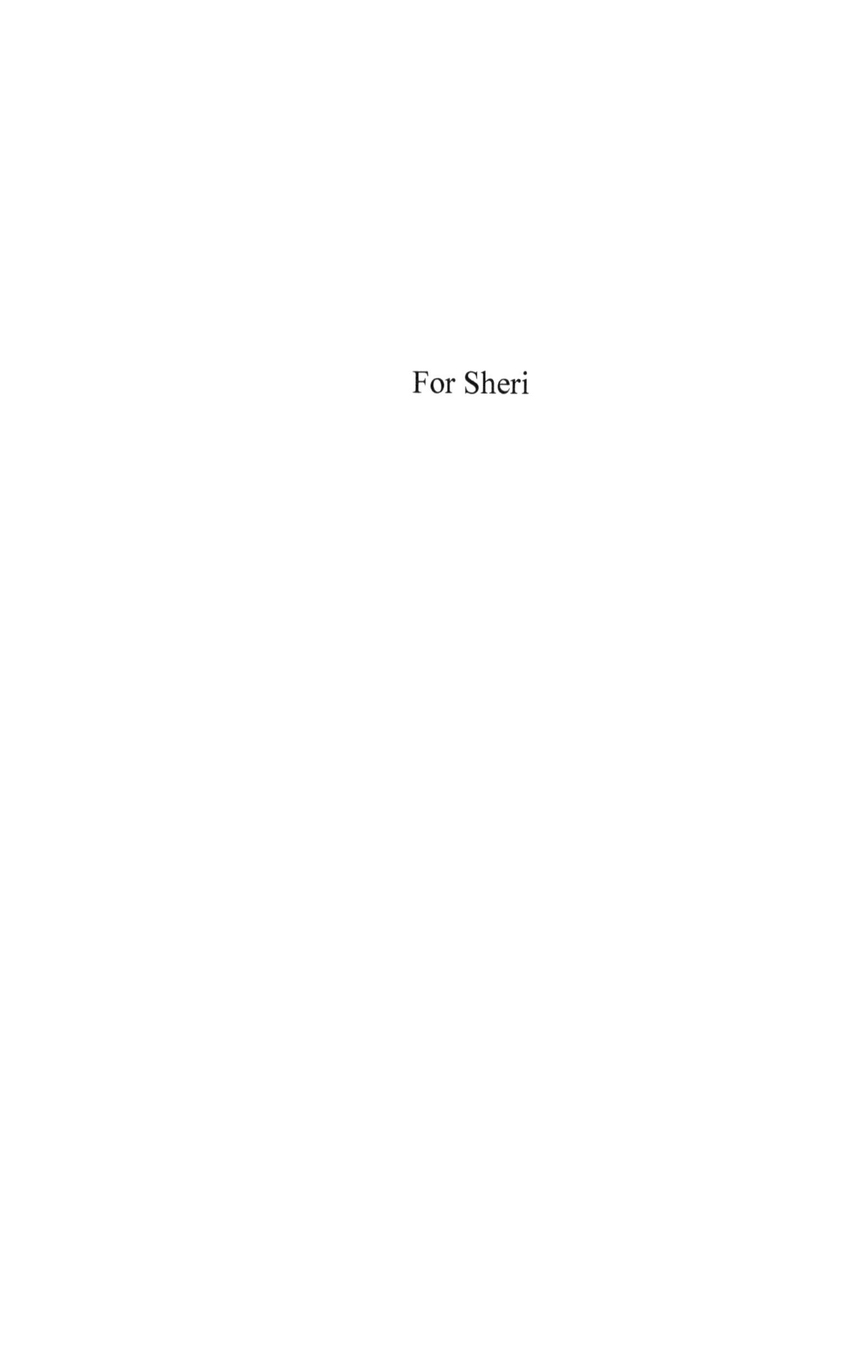
For Sheri

ISBN 978-1-4477-2628-9

CHAPTERS

KICK-OFF

When Sheri and I flew out of Adelaide in early 2007 it was the first time since 1983 we'd travelled as a couple. There had been many trips with the boys and we'd even made solo journeys, but this was, in its way, a new experience.

The plan was to visit Yemen, Lebanon, Syria, Jordan, Oman and the United Arab Emirates. A wind-down week in Bangkok would make the trip about seven and a half weeks long.

We had a one-night stopover in Bangkok to break the journey, landing in the late evening. A taxi whizzed us at 120 kph along the expressway towards the city centre. I had to direct the driver the last bit of the way, but by midnight we were at the New Siam 2 in Banglamphu, my hotel from a trip three years ago.

The foyer was warm and humid. Two women were washing the floor with old rags. The place didn't look its best at this time of night—it was better in the day time when it was alive with people. Never mind. Time for a sleep.

I woke early, feeling okay after yesterday's long flight. Sheri slept on while I went for a walk around the area, a favourite with backpackers. Already the fragrant air was heavy in the narrow laneways, lined with funky 70's-style restaurants, shops and hotels. These parallel lanes all terminated in one long cross-street, edged with little food stalls. A high wall along its far side marked the limit of a large wat beyond, spread out among tall trees. The screech of cockerels made it clear that the monks kept chickens.

I walked around the wat's perimeter to Khao San Road, a small but notorious street. At night it teemed with travelers and was crassly, noisily commercial. But at this early hour it was almost empty, except for Thai workers picking up rubbish bags to dump into trailers. They were careful not to disturb a local man, sleeping flat on his back on the pavement

In one of the many restaurants near the New Siam 2 I had breakfast, taking in the relaxed atmosphere and slightly decrepit feel of the place. When I got back to the hotel Sheri was awake and dressed, so we went out for a look around together.

We walked through the wat, where a ceremony was in progress in the temple. A voice droned monotonously while camera crews filmed the audience. We left, and Sheri had her breakfast in a restaurant funky with plants, old cane chairs, and fish in a pool.

Later we had some time to pass before catching our plane to Dubai, so we took a tourist boat down the Chao Phraya, the big river that bisects Bangkok. But at the last stop we had to get straight back on a return ferry—the trip had taken longer than expected. We picked up our bags from the hotel and grabbed a taxi to the airport, in time for the six and a half hour flight to Dubai. We had a three-day stopover there before going on to Yemen.

The plane landed at 9.30 pm local time and we caught a cab to our hotel, booked over the internet just like Bangkok.

It was good to know exactly where you were staying when you arrived in a city at night and Sheri was skilful at finding a place.

This one was a replica of a traditional Arab house, large, plain and white. The room was meant for a family and was enormous, with high ceilings. There was a king-size bed. The doors were solid timber and the windows were barred. There were no curtains, but the shutters were as heavy as stable doors. Yet this was all upstairs and inside a large building.

Again I woke early and left Sheri asleep. I walked along "The Creek" as the locals call the wide sea inlet to Dubai. There was a long bank of dhows, the trucks of the coastal trade, jammed together by the hundreds. Cargo was piled along the wharf next to the road, ready for loading.

None of these boats had the traditional masts, relying instead on engines. The men aboard were a friendly lot and cheerfully let me take photographs.

Sheri and I went out later and this time walked all day, mostly seeing reconstructions of older Dubai buildings. One aspect was the old-time wind-towers, ingenious four-sided structures that stood above houses to draw up the hot air and cool them. Alternatively, depending on wind conditions, they could drive cooler air down into the buildings. These were made of stone in the more solid houses, but even the reed houses of fishermen could have a wind tower made of poles and sacking.

My main image of Dubai that day was of the tight ranks of dhows, piled with cargo, against a background of large, ultra-modern buildings. Small ferries called "abras" thud-thudded to and fro across the river, carrying passengers sitting on low, flat cabin roofs. Each boat had a fixed awning for shade. A trip cost one dirham, about thirty cents.

Tired, fairly hot, we went back to the hotel for the evening. I opened the first small bottle of a six-pack of Famous Grouse whiskey, on duty-free special in Melbourne airport— my rations for the 'dry' countries that lay in front of us.

We slept till around nine, having got up in the small hours to hush some loudly-talking night staff and friends. Breakfast was a fairly dismal omelette and brown bread when the restaurant opened at ten, with coffee super-sweet from condensed milk.

A taxi took us to the biggest, grandest shopping centre in Dubai. Here the local ladies and girls swished around in their elegant burquas, mixing with more informally dressed local women and European expats. There is a Ugandan population, which probably explained why I saw a number of black women, usually quite striking and dramatically dressed. Even I was able to find a few interesting things in the shops, mainly antique rifles, though not in very good shape.

More unusual were giant star-wars type monsters made of old car parts. They were amazingly intricate, elaborately fashioned from lots of engine parts including con-rods, pistons, spark plugs and bits I didn't recognize. At $8,000 they seemed like fair value for the enormous labour and skill involved. Bit bizarre for the front room at home, though.

We took a bus back to our hotel area, which we found without getting lost more than once. We made a return reservation for the hotel for April and got a good discount. Tomorrow we would be up early for a taxi to Sharjah Airport, en route to Saan'a in Yemen. That's where the real adventure would start.

YEMEN

Arabian Airlines left an hour late, but the plane was modern. Now, suddenly, there were women everywhere, but mostly in burquas. They were not as shy as I had expected. One, in the departure lounge of Sharjah Airport, took out her breast to feed her child, quite openly.

We were met at Saan'a by a man and a teenager from the hotel. The driver was in a hurry—he'd been waiting two hours. He hustled us into an old Toyota Landcruiser, saying: "No time to change money! Must go!"

Saan'a is on a plateau surrounded by dry, rugged mountains. The road was full of honking, aggressively-driven vehicles, jostling and pushing, obeying no rules at all. Our driver, a bit of a ruffian with a kanjar, the traditional Arab dagger in his belt, enjoyed himself in the hurly-burley. He was pleased by our seeming lack of concern, but the truth was that Sheri thought he would only be spurred on if we did show it. Besides, I wouldn't give him the satisfaction of thinking he'd scared us.

"Australians good!" he said. "French people make noise like girls!" He made squealing-in-fright noises, like a little pig. I couldn't help smiling.

The road led through very poor buildings on both sides, along with straggling street stalls. Poverty and roughness dominated. We began to see the multi-storied, mud-brick and stone buildings for which Saan'a is known, but so far this was the most confronting shambles of a city that I had seen in a very long time. A warm, pleasant feeling spread through me. "I'm somewhere!" I thought.

Further in, the buildings were around four to six stories high, a medium brown in colour, with the storey levels marked with white square patterns. The windows appeared to be roughly plastered in arch-shapes around rectangular glass, again all in white. They looked like big, square, wedding cakes. We'd never seen anything like it.

We pulled in at the hotel where a large camel lay outside, almost like a parked car. The building was similar to all the others, with the first several stories made of square stone blocks and the upper ones of mud brick. High, steep steps led to the first floor.

We stooped before a five-foot doorway to open a pair of narrow, wooden doors, giving just enough room to enter. The room was of medium size, gleaming white, and very rustic in construction. The floor sloped down several degrees, like a mildly-listing boat. There were four windows in the end wall. The top two were roughly arched and were filled with what looked like translucent animal skin, though it was a hard substance, possibly mineral. The bottom pair was rectangular and had pairs of opening glass doors with wooden frames.

We made coffee in our electric jug nicknamed "Birko", which Sheri had taken to Africa. Then into the streets and a rougher, wilder place I had never seen and (other than the slums of India) never a poorer one.

The Yemeni equivalent of siesta was on. Everyone had stopped work and most people were chewing hugely-fat cheekfuls of qat, a mild narcotic. Muslims don't drink, but here they had a substitute. There were some women beggars, one with three children lying in a neat bed on the pavement. Did they lie quietly all day? It looked like it.

We went into a military museum, full of weapons and pictures of the revolution of the sixties, especially pictures of "martyrs" being beheaded. There were motor cars—bullet-proof Cadillacs of former leaders and a charming black Morris 10, vintage 1940's, from the days of the British Protectorate of Aden.

Bangkok was a world away and Dubai just a fading memory in the face of this place. Gone were the immaculate white robes, the black and white head-gear of Dubai Arabs. Here the costume for the men was old western-style jackets over shabby robes, with curved kanjars stuck in waist bands. The poorest of street stalls cluttered the roads, with seriously-battered 70's Toyota taxis honking their way through.

Our mobiles wouldn't work. But there were internet cafes even here: rough establishments set amongst the general squalor, but cheap and with surprisingly fast connections.

That evening the call to prayer from the mosque outside our window was very loud. I imagined how it might be at 4 a.m. There was a hubbub of voices nearby. Sleep would be broken tonight, most likely. We walked back to the large square in the town and ate in a restaurant where some other Europeans sat, along with locals. The food was meat and rice, crudely prepared and cooked, but tasty.

Later we walked through residential alleys behind the hotel. These were narrow, cobbled lanes through the multi-storied buildings, all probably hundreds of years old. This was very different from the scruffy commercial area.

We came across another hotel, one that Sheri had read about, and asked to see a room. After that we were politely shown up to the roof of the six-storey building, climbing steadily up the steep, stone stairs. Seated comfortably in the evening air, we enjoyed cold, refreshing drinks. The views were superb, extending over the city to the faraway hills.

I'd heard muezzins before, but these Yemenis took first prize. The local guy started up at 4 a.m. and just kept right on going. I could hear the more distant ones, rather like cats calling to each other. But all that didn't wake Sheri. She slept on, obliviously.

Later we spent the morning wandering in the quarter where we had been last night, mostly in the souk. Brightly coloured goods lined the alleys, where black-clad women moved among the more shabbily-dressed men.

Through an open door Sheri saw a camel inside a large, sombre room. It was blinkered and walked in circles to power an ancient, wooden oil-press. The young fellow in charge was friendly to us and we entered the gloom to take a couple of pictures.

Back at the hotel we arranged with the same man who'd brought us from the airport to take a five-day drive. Later we had dinner at the hotel where we'd visited last evening. Once again we climbed the very high steps to the roof, but this time we had the camera to shoot the views across the buildings to the surrounding mountains.

Repeated loud banging at the hotel's front gate woke us in the small hours.

"Yallah, yallah!" (Go away! Get out of here!) called the hotel custodian, sounding very irritated.

It was something to do with the very early departure of a group of package tourists. We'd been surprised at breakfast to find that the other guests were fairly elderly, some very much so. This wasn't an easy country to travel in, nor a particularly safe one. Where were the adventurous young travelers?

The hotel restaurant was open only for breakfasts because of rebuilding. It was in the open air and the food was served buffet-style, mostly Arab bread with jams or cheese and boiled eggs, with coffee and fruit. Swarms of flies were trying to get into the jam or honey, with a fair rate of success. There were portable fans set up to blow them away, but these blew over the tables of the nearest guests, so people turned the fans away. This made it easy for the flies!

We left with our driver, Mohammed. About forty-five, he wore a turban, the usual jacket over a robe, and the kanjar he'd had at the airport. He looked fairly tough and capable. Today he had a newer Landcruiser. It cost US$60 per day all up, a good price.

We drove out on the road that the hotel fronted. This was really a viaduct well below the level of the areas it ran through. In the winter it flowed with water. In the summer it flowed with cars.

Soon enough we left the city and entered harsh, mountainous country, more jagged rock than earth. First stop was Wadi Dhakr, only fourteen kilometres from Saan'a. This is best known for the Dar-al-Hajar, an imam's palace. It was the typical multi-storied elaborate stone structure, but built on a mushroom-shaped rock pillar, very dramatic. Inside, wells ran down so deep we had no chance of seeing the bottom. Getting water out of those couldn't have been easy.

On a lower level, outside the main palace, a family with a very old lady in tow seemed to want something. The old woman, made up with green paint below her eyes, was so taken by Sheri's eyes that she kissed her hand, which left Sheri disconcerted at moments during the rest of the day. Mohammed couldn't shed any light on it.

On one of the upper levels another family included an ancient woman so shrunken that she looked a hundred years old. Yet she had climbed many stairs, quite high ones. Or perhaps she'd been carried.

Walking back to the car we passed through a little farming village. Many of its structures, including walls, were mud-brick. Even so close to Saan'a, we were amongst traditional people.

From Wadi Dhakr we went to Thula, an historic fortified village. Once again the houses were of the high, stone-walled type. Some were very elaborate, with round windows of brick and triangular ends of stone projecting in patterns. One of these had patterns of the Star of David and had been a Jewish house. But the Jews were gone and no Muslim would live in such a house. So it stood empty, and may have done for centuries.

Huge, broad cisterns held most of the town's water supply, but we were told the water was not drinkable, even though it came from the mountains very close to the town.

We had a good lunch at a roadside restaurant, shared with Mohammed—fresh, flat bread, roast chicken and a pot of thick, spicy soup served in the hot, heavy iron platter in which it had been cooked. Then on to a fairly scruffy town called Shibam where we would see a busy market tomorrow. The elevation was 2,300 metres and the air was cool. We walked part way up a steep path lined with numerous small excavated caves. We were told these were prehistoric houses, but they looked like tombs to me.

High above we could see a few buildings. Later we spent half an hour driving up to these, which were part of a village called Kawkaban. Fairly insignificant now, with many of the small, loose-laid stone houses in disrepair, it had once been an important place. At 3,000 metres high, it had sweeping views for many kilometres around.

We stood on one of the cliff edges looking down at Shibam, seven hundred metres below. Though the cliff was sheer where we stood, tomorrow we would walk down a path leading down from another part of the village to the market in Shibam. The car would be there waiting.

I wasn't too sure about walking down the path to far-below Shibam. Too much scrambling down a really rough path would be tough on my dodgy left knee. But the steep upper part was well made and only the gentler, lower part was rough.

The busy market sold mainly food: vegetables, spices and meat, usually with the animal's head on display. Perhaps this showed what a healthy beast it had been.

It was a swirling, noisy market that was easy to enjoy. As we got to the end of things we saw Mohammed waiting by the car further down the street.

Soon we were approaching another town. I began to think: "Seen one, seen them all!" However when we got there we saw in front of us a wonderfully clear, large cistern. Contained by a hand-smoothed plaster wall, the water looked about three metres deep with green plants growing right up from the bottom. It seemed to be a mini eco-system, about sixty metres across. Women came and filled containers; some boys came to play.

The lads were a cheerful group and said "Soura, soura, khalam, khalam," to us. We knew by now that this meant "Take a picture of us and give us pens." We did. Later we bought dozens of pens to give away—all the children wanted them.

The Toyota climbed steeply up to around the 3,000 metre level, far above the broad valley floors, back up to the mountain peaks and a plateau. At the top, an old, rough, stone fortress-house perched on a promontory. Its walls were flush with the perpendicular rock, falling sheer for at least three hundred metres. Mohammed led the way in and slipped some money to the handful of people who lived there.

They led us through a narrow alleyway and up a steep, stone path or stairway. On one side was a rock wall, on the other, just a metre or so away, a vertical drop, which—if you fell—would give you plenty of time to consider your fate as you plummeted down. The trick, I told Sheri, was to look only at the safe inward wall, for vertigo was a real risk. I could feel it myself and took my own advice.

There was a bit of a scramble to get to a flat roof which Sheri and I succeeded in well enough, but Mohammed needed a hand up. The reward was a panorama vaster than I had ever seen. This tiny but spectacular place was called Zacatee.

Later, at a roadside restaurant, our driver called for a similar feast to yesterday's. The whole thing for the three of us cost about $11.

The good road gave way to a rough track under construction, and then to a road in the very early stages of being built. Here the Landcruiser came into its own, especially where the ground was deeply boggy. Mohammed was a careful, skilful driver, in spite of his cavalier attitude when driving in from the airport, and eased the big car through everything.

We climbed again to a harsh, rocky plateau and turned onto a barely-discernible track. Even here were tiny patches of slightly-tilled ground where people literally scraped a living. Just short of another precipitous drop and another grand panorama, Mohammed stopped the car. He greeted two old, bearded men who seemed to be just sitting contemplating the view, perched on the cliff-edge. I sat down (it felt a lot safer) with my feet sticking over the edge. One of the old men shouted in my ear. I guessed he was deaf.

A huge valley stretched out before us, broad, deep and stretching away into the distance. The view was different from the one at Kawkaban or Zacatee. What looked like erosion was in fact a vast system of terraces, lines of loose-laid rock walls with soil built up behind them. They were like little dams, but full of light-coloured soil. The longer I looked the more I saw. There were broad terraces on the gentler side of the great valley, but multitudes of very narrow ones on the steeper side. Later we saw many more of these terraces, probably the accumulated work of hundreds of years.

In the centre of all this, but on the flatter side of the valley, I gradually discerned houses, some green trees and even some green patches of terrace. The scene was so beautiful, so subtly complex, that I sat for a long time, not distracted by the strong smell of urine coming from the old men, who sat contented in each other's company.

Driving on, we returned to the road and soon picked up three walkers, members of a "Hash Harriers Club" from Saan'a, all of whom spoke English. Further on, Mohammed stopped the car and the rest of us got out and walked to the next town. This looked like a crusader castle. Outbuildings sprawled across the landscape. We could have stayed there, but chose to carry on.

Gradually we entered fertile country where greenery, trees and vegetable patches became the norm. We reached the large town of Al Maheet and here our driver took us to a good hotel, for which Sheri and I were thankful after the one at Kawkaban.

Mohammed did a deal of some sort at the hotel desk. When I tried to check on the price he gently stood on my foot, so I shut up and left it to him. We learned that we could trust him—even if he was skimming a bit off the top, we were still getting a good deal.

So much had been packed into the two days since we left Saan'a. So much since we had left Adelaide only one week ago: Bangkok, Dubai, Saan'a, and now these last two days. What a contrast with an ordinary week in Adelaide! It wasn't an overload, but it sure was maximum experiential input.

This morning we drove out of the hotel and very soon turned onto a rough track. This led to another amazing view, with great ridges falling away. There were wave-like peaks on these with one side very steep and the other more gradual. Each peak had a tiny village perched on it. It was like a scene from "Lord of the Rings" in its stern grandeur. We could hear the sounds of roosters and children floating up towards us. There was almost no sign of the modern world—the place was from another time.

Back in Maheet Mohammed dropped us near the ancient top of the town. We had walked up to it last evening. It was truly medieval, with a narrow entrance gate passing under the walls. Two very cheerful boys showed us around—they knew what we would find interesting. Old wooden doors, mostly only about 1.2 metres high, a carved statue of David on one door, a house uninhabited because of "djinnies", or ghosts. They also showed us their decrepit sandals, asked us for 200 rials each, (about a dollar) and danced with joy when they got it.

Mohammed drove down to the beginning of a wadi, where the road was just a rocky riverbed. We drove a long way along this track, occasionally sandy. It was much warmer at this lower altitude—the flat fringes were fertile with vegetables, banana palms, mango trees, coffee beans and the inevitable qat.

The people here were different. The women wore bright clothes of yellow, orange, green and purple. Some of them wore fitted dresses, not burquas, and many did not wear the veil.

We picked up a passenger, who scrambled up onto the roof rack. He got a very bumpy ride at times, but I supposed that was normal.

We passed wells, donkeys, cattle and goats. In places a channel of water ran along the riverbed, but otherwise it was dry.

Once again, Sheri and I got out and walked while the car went ahead. People greeted us, though some women were shy. There was nothing predictable about this—other women were friendly, burquas or not.

We rejoined the vehicle, which eventually left the wadi and climbed out of the warm valleys back into the cooler, misty high altitudes. At a place called Manaka we stopped. This, it seemed, was a base for walking to nearby villages. But to our dismay, the town was very dirty, with lots of dust and rubbish. In one place raw sewage spilled across the road and the smell was rank.

The hotel, by contrast, was very decent, more of a traditional "fondouk". It had a name fit to bring joy to the owner: the El Hajarah Tourist Hotel. Our room was large and airy with lots of lacework plaster decorations framing the upper windows, which were the usual arches with coloured glass in ornate patterns—lead-light, Arab style. Wooden-shuttered windows framed most of the walls on two sides, overlooking the valley. There was no furniture except five single mattresses on the carpeted floor. In all, a very pleasant room, painted white, with colourful curtains. The odd bed-bug merely added to the authenticity, but I was scratching bites in the morning.

Dinner was included in the hotel tariff and Mohammed came to get us at seven. In the basement was a very large room of traditional style, with a carpeted floor and cushions all round the walls. An absolute feast of many dishes was put before us, which we could not possibly have finished, so I invited Mohamed to join us. A dozen Norwegians came in and we chatted to some of them.

After dinner a group of traditional musicians and dancers entertained us. They got some of the tourists up to dance, including Sheri. The manager of the hotel, a large and jolly man, was an accomplished dancer. Sheri sat down, but he soon got her up again. She had done some belly-dancing years ago and easily fitted into the rhythm.

It was a good evening, even though the power failed and the lights went out. Candles were produced and the musicians never missed a beat.

Sheri and I sat side by side and Mohammed sat on my left. He and I were developing an understanding where a look conveyed more than half-understood words.

On Sheri's right a youngish, fit-looking Norwegian engaged her in eager conversation. He said he had travelled alone across Nepal using satellite maps and a GPS. A pleasant, articulate man, he seemed to latch on to Sheri, perhaps because the rest of his group was much older than him.

Mohammed gestured to me, making a duck-quacking movement with his fingers, and jerked his head towards the Norwegian.

"Is that good man?" he asked.

"Yes, he's fine," I said. "He is not making Ali Babas with my wife." (Ali Baba was a joke Mohammed liked to make about thieves) But now Mohammed pulled out his dagger.

"Sheree is like sister to me!"

I explained that men could talk to women in my country and that the husband had to judge if it was OK or not. (Not that I let Sheri hear me say that!)

Mohammed settled down. He hadn't been serious about the knife, I thought, but he had become protective.

Next day we drove to a small hill-top village some kilometres away. Mohammed had arranged a guide to lead us on a three or four hour walk to another village. It was hard going, mostly uphill, over rough and rocky tracks. Of course there were wonderful views. The steeper, higher and rougher the promontory the more likely it was to have a fortified village perched atop.

The guide led us into one of these little villages through a typical gate—an arch through the outer and inner wall, a distance of perhaps three metres. The low roof between the arches was supported by logs, with wattle and daub between. There would be a room directly overhead because the multi-storied houses themselves formed the secure outer wall. For this reason there were no accessible windows on the lower levels outside.

As we were leaving, our guide (who spoke no English) suggested we take tea. So we entered a private house and climbed up some perfectly-smooth, mud-brick stairs. We took off our shoes and walked into a medium-sized, white-washed room. Once again, it was edged with cushions on the floor and back cushions against the walls. There were a few ornaments on the wall, including a ceremonial dagger and sash. A little boy sat watching Mickey Mouse on a small cable TV.

The owner brought us in tea—it was a tiny, home-based business—and sat to talk with the guide. He also spoke little or no English. When we were finished I began to move and the owner quickly stood.

We paid for the tea and carried on. The going was still hard, but we had water, bananas and bread and stopped for a rest as necessary. At last we began to go down, in company with a small herd of goats, a shepherd boy and a fierce dog.

I slipped on a loose, sandy patch and came down with a hard bump, but no harm was done. The long descent was hard on my knees. But at last we reached our destination and were led into a hotel foyer, where we gratefully sat on two plastic chairs. Ten minutes later Mohammed arrived with the Toyota.

Next morning we drove back to Saan'a. What had we seen of danger or violence in Yemen? Not much. People were very easy-going and comradely. A few young men sported old AK47's. Several times we saw modern 4WD pick-ups with heavy-calibre machine guns mounted in the back and half a dozen smartly-uniformed soldiers to man them. There were police control points on the roads, but we never had to show our passports, thanks to our driver's glib tongue. We would not have been allowed to enter the genuinely dangerous areas.

We passed through a fairly remote region before we got to Saan'a.

"Peoples here sell whiskey, beer, hashish," said Mohammed.

"How is that possible?" Sheri asked.

"Mafia!"

Mohammed had said there were no Ali Babas in Yemen. But as we re-entered the city we saw some police roughly leading a man away, closely followed by excited locals. Mohammed said he was a thief who would probably get a month or two in jail.

Back at the Felix Arabia hotel in the old quarter, we thanked Mohammed and tipped him well. He'd done a good job.

We went out into the scruffy market area. Somehow it seemed cleaner and not so wild. It looked familiar now. We walked straight past the woman with the three drugged children, neatly laid out sleeping, and headed for the email café. We'd acclimatized.

In the evening we revisited the big souk. It was different at night, brightly lit, and we found sections we'd missed before. There were specific areas for different products. One alley was full of gleaming brasswork, another of ornate daggers and sheaths. We fossicked around until Sheri bought some clove oil, which the vendor got by climbing a ladder to the top shelf, at ceiling level. With this she cured smelly sandals!

That was our last night in Yemen. We'd seen a lot and were ready to go. We wouldn't forget the powerful scenery, the honking traffic, the sociable men with qat-bulging cheeks, the small, black-clad women who could surprise you with sudden friendliness. And the frequent greeting: "Welcome to Yemen!"

We left Saan'a by the road in front of the hotel that so much resembled a viaduct and did carry up to three metres of water in winter. Near the airport soldiers stopped to check us. One of them greeted Mohammed affectionately and kissed him on both cheeks.

"A friend? A cousin?" I asked. He laughed: "Many friends!"

We farewelled warmly. It had taken us a while to really trust him, and he was probably a bit of a rascal. But he had treated us well.

* * * * * *

Sharjah, just north of Dubai, was the hub through which Air Arabia operated. It was ten hours before the next flight to Beirut, so we had arranged to stay overnight. The hotel was clean and modern, run by a sleekly-handsome Indian. No bed bugs here!

Like Dubai, Sharjah is on the coast and has a large sea-inlet, called the lagoon. Many of the dhows still had their traditional, long lateen-rigged booms slung from the short, forward-canting masts. Also as in Dubai, the men working on them were friendly and some invited me to take pictures. Nearby was a souk, a big market full of all sorts of fish. Fishermen unloaded their flapping catch over the sea wall. At one end a shed was full of men who gutted and cleaned the fish people had bought.

Wandering back through large, green parks and Gulf-style modern buildings designed for size and appearance, Sheri spent time in a multi-storey arcade full of carpets, supposedly-antique jewellery and clothing. In one I found a genuine old sextant, but elsewhere others were fake. The place was geared towards tourists and practically everything "old" was reproduction.

The area around the hotel was mostly Indian. Dinner was in a traditional Indian restaurant with big, steaming plates of chicken biryani and mughla. Some people used cutlery, some didn't. Back in the hotel we had an undisturbed sleep, the windows keeping out the morning call to prayer from the adjacent mosque amplifiers.

The morning taxi probably ripped us off, because the fare was almost double what the hotel manager had predicted. On the freeway the driver hit 140 kph, only slightly faster than the other cars! Then we were back at Sharjah Airport, en route to Beirut.

LEBANON

Around 3pm local time we passed over snow-capped mountains and landed in Beirut. We weren't sure what we we'd find in terms of it being a fairly recent war zone. If it was bad, we'd leave.

The Hotel New Talal, recommended by Lonely Planet, was a poor start.

A scruffy dump, so shabby as to be almost beyond description, it was not a place we wanted to stay. But nearby was the Pension Al Nazih, much better. We registered, filling in our mothers and fathers' first names as required. Dubious logic there!

A short walk took us into the new city, the re-built centre near the waterfront. This consisted of beautiful, multi-storied sandstone buildings, with French balconies and shutters. These lined a broad mall. There were many restaurants, but very few people.

Nearby, a young Moslem man, probably a student, showed us a beautiful mosque. He explained that it had been a crusader church. Repairs to recent war damage had revealed a Roman temple beneath that. Layer upon layer of history …

Not far away was another ancient building, an Orthodox church. The ceiling and wall frescoes were ornate and looked pagan by comparison with the simple austerity of the mosque.

We wandered up the lovely mall, past the empty restaurants with lots of outside seating. It was only about four-thirty—perhaps it was just too early for the locals. As it was, soldiers outnumbered the few pedestrians. It was impossible to ignore the military presence, especially when a convoy raced up the mall. All the same, we ate well, then returned to the *pension* and the heavy-eyed boy who cleaned the floors. But mostly, it seemed, he squatted on the stairs and smoked cigarettes while playing on a game-boy.

Other travellers were in the *pension*: a big, elderly Canadian and some backpackers. A pleasant, attractive woman ran the place and made sure it was immaculate. To the point of obsession we found out later!

On the way to the National Museum next day we passed several tanks and armoured troop carriers stationed at various points. The soldiers here looked tough and professional.

The museum had an impressive collection of large statues and sarcophagi, all Hellenic. The smaller artifacts, however, were much earlier.

A video was interesting because it showed the museum's restoration after the civil war. Then it had been a ruined shell. The statues and other objects had been encased in reinforced concrete at the beginning of the war and had been jack-hammered out later. The concrete meant that bored soldiers had been unable to do significant damage, but water had affected many stored items. It had been a wet, broken mess and gave some idea of the effects of war.

A bus took us to Hamra, next to the city centre, and we walked along the corniche, or seafront. Rebuilding was happening everywhere, but the twisted, open faces of some large buildings remained. Mostly, police kept people away, but I was allowed to photograph one.

That evening we went to an English pub, "The Bulldog". The owners were two long-time expats, both engaging characters. Stuart was a half-Lebanese Scot who worked as a photo-journalist. He looked odd—a classic Scot, but with a very dark complexion. He told us he had taken most photos of the war, both here and in Iraq, that had been shown in "The Australian" newspaper.

Keith, a lean, fair-haired Englishman, had lived in Beirut for twelve years. He loved the vitality of the city. Life for him was a series of financial ups and downs, but he was optimistic about Beirut's recovery.

Three slow pints of Murphy's Stout later, (the last bought by Keith) we left. He'd told us a lot about Lebanon, some of which we'd put to use tomorrow.

A series of buses took us the forty five kilometres north to Byblos. Traffic honked as the road led past scruffy apartment buildings, never far from the coast. These began to give way to a more resort-like environment as Beirut was left behind.

Eventually, we were in open country. At a place called Nahr al Kalb we got off the bus to look for some historic graffiti Keith had told us about. There was a high bluff overlooking the sea and a river running near one side. A narrow road ran between the hill and the river.

As we walked along we saw a series of carvings and plaques set along the bottom of the hill. The first few of these, several feet high, were formal commemorations of the liberation of Lebanon in the first and second world wars by allied armies. These were only mildly interesting to us—we were after more heavy-duty stuff.

A path led upwards, blocked by a locked gate. However, somebody had bent back a bar and I thought I could squeeze through. To Sheri's surprise, I did, so she followed.

Now we saw no more militaristic inscriptions. Instead ancient, eroded figures were carved into the rock. One was from Rameses II in 1270 BC. Now *that* was impressive! Another was by a king of the Assyrians who had later ruled this region.

This was very ancient stuff and we had it to ourselves. We had climbed hundreds of feet above the sea and the view was wonderful, which was no doubt why the site had been chosen by the ancients. There was a sense of timelessness looking out from that place, all the more so because it seemed to have been forgotten.

Back at the gate I had real difficulty getting through. The angle was wrong. An image of being stuck for hours crossed my mind as I tried again. Very gradually, however, I squeezed through. It was a bit scary for a little while!

It was easy to flag down another bus and the ride was very cheap. Soon Byblos came into sight. We walked down the little streets and had coffee and sandwiches before tackling the ruins. Most of it was in a pretty bad state, but the crusader castle still stood, massive and proud.

Much older, however, were underground tombs. They were about seven metres square and cut about nine metres

deep, straight down through the rock. At the bottom of each tomb, one side was dug out to contain a sarcophagus.
Some were still there, either in place or lifted out onto the ground above.

Remains of Roman pillars stood around a small amphitheatre overlooking the sea, which also gave the sense of timelessness. We were just two more people in an endless stream, enjoying the view like all the generations before us.

Other pillars had been sliced up like sausages and used end-on in the bottom parts of the crusader castle walls. They looked like circular grey patches against the lighter-coloured blocks. Some of the rectangular blocks were huge, as much as five metres long.

There is a lovely little port at Byblos and the seawall protecting it is crusader-built, also using sections of Roman pillars set end-on horizontally into the wall. Sheri went to look at the shops while I pottered around the port.

The bus home dropped us at its terminus and we caught a taxi the rest of the way. The driver spoke fairly good English.

"Lebanon is no good for work now. Where you from? Australia? Perfect! Listen, you get me on plane, I drive you everywhere you want, free!"

Baalbeck was next, in the Bekaa Valley. Hezbollah territory. A taxi took us to the bus terminal, a place called Cola, where mini-buses vied for our business. The vehicles were about equally decrepit, especially the seats. We climbed aboard one. As soon as it was reasonably full we were off, climbing up into the mountains, with apartment blocks lining the road.

The engine roared and raced—the pace was fast. Soon the snowy mountain peaks looked much closer. We swerved around potholes, obstructions and diversions, rattling and thumping our way past soldiers and armoured vehicles. At one point we diverted down a valley to cross a river. Beside us soared a huge, modern suspension bridge, very fine—except for a large hole, blasted neatly through the middle of its roadway by devastatingly- accurate Israeli bombing.

Two hours later we were in Baalbeck. It was a scruffy little town. The ruins, however, were extensive and impressive, far more so than in Byblos. The main structures were Roman. Most magnificent was the enormous temple of Bacchus with its soaring pillars, and walls, still standing almost intact. But there were few other visitors besides us. The war had ruined tourism.

As we left we were offered Hezbollah T-shirts and flags, which we declined. Not ideal to re-enter Australia sporting pro-Hezbollah emblems!

The bus home was even faster and more erratic than the first. We passed two Hezbollah parades marching along the road. Once back at the terminus we caught another taxi, but when we got out the driver wanted fifteen thousand lira—double the usual fee. I refused and gave him seven. His protests earned him one thousand more, which left us both happy enough.

Sheri and I checked out the bus station for our trip north tomorrow, out of Lebanon to the Krak des Chevaliers in Syria. This was the largest, most imposing crusader castle ever built, and T. E. Lawrence's favourite. I was looking forward to it.

Back at the *pension*, we had got used to the constant washing and cleaning of floors and furniture from morning until late evening, done by the long-suffering staff. The proprietress had seemed to grow more stressed each day. One afternoon we had come back to a flood running into the street, but it was only the stairs being hosed down.

That night we had a really good dinner in the new city centre and talked about what we'd seen. We had found Lebanon to be a fairly frantic place. Perhaps it had always been so, or maybe it was the war.

Up quite early, we collected a pillow case full of clean, folded washing from the staff. We packed, very much a routine by now. Each of us had a medium-sized rucksack with wheels and an extending handle. We carried a small day-bag on our backs, which doubled as cabin luggage on planes. The system worked well.

Ten minutes of trundling the rucksacks got us to the state-run bus station. At 10 a.m. we rolled out, aboard a large, luxurious bus. The ride was comfortable and easy, unlike the chaotic rush of yesterday. Gradually the coast took on more and more of a natural look, especially after Byblos. It must all have been like this when had I hitchhiked southwards forty-plus years ago.

Still, Tripoli was now, as Keith had said, all apartment blocks. We stopped for a while to pick up passengers before carrying on. The other passengers, all Syrian, seemed a friendly, homely lot, more relaxed than the Lebanese.

SYRIA

Once through the formalities of the Syrian frontier the landscape changed very quickly. Aridity gave way to green hills and fields, even while the snow-clad mountain hinterland of Lebanon was still visible.

We asked the driver to drop us at a place where we could catch a cab to the Krak. He dropped us on the roadside by a turn-off, seemingly in the middle of nowhere. But, sooner than we thought likely, a small yellow taxi came along. The driver was very relaxed, although his car was neither old nor shabby. We put our gear in the boot and told him we wanted to go to the Hotel Bibars. I asked him how much. “Taxi”, he replied calmly. “Bibars”. As if, what more needs to be said?

We drove slowly along, more or less uphill, until we passed a few flat-roofed houses, then came to the hotel. It was well-appointed and the room had a balcony looking directly onto the magnificent grey-white castle, which lay just across a small valley. We were delighted.

Later, although too late to enter the castle, we walked round the head of the valley and around part of the vast castle. The people we met confirmed our brief impression that, at least so far, Syrians were relaxed and friendly.

Dinner was at a large and well-built restaurant near the castle. Platter after platter of mezes arrived, with roast chicken and a glass of local red wine. Outside, the wind boomed and buffeted—Syria was cooler than Lebanon.

The owner sat down with us after dinner, a very decent man, but a frustrated one.

"The government won't let me add a storey to the building to take in guests," he complained. "They don't look after the castle. I want European tourists here. Arabs are much too fussy, wanting this and that all the time." (We had been waited on hand and foot)

As we left he said, "Sean Connery had dinner here in 2000. Want to see his signature?" We did, and a characterful one it looked. Then we walked into the starry but dark night, to find our way back to our hotel past fiercely-barking dogs. We each kept a stone ready in our hands, but didn't need them.

Entrance to the Krak was three dollars each, ridiculously cheap. For once we took a guide, at six dollars also cheap. The castle was enormous from the outside, but inside it was simply vast. There were vaulted stables where hundreds of horses had been kept. Soldiers had slept on a mezzanine floor above, warmed in winter by the body heat of the horses. The gigantic circular oven had fed four thousand soldiers and four hundred knights.

From the highest ramparts you could see for perhaps fifty kilometers. Tripoli was still in view.

Living in the castle must have been like living in a town, it was so big and complex. It was very easy to get lost — when the guide left us, we did just that.

As we were leaving, a local tout tried to sell us some of his wares. He was very pressing, almost frantic in his manner. Sheri did want to buy some more slide film, so looked at two that he had. But the boxes had been glued together so no-one could see the expiry dates! He objected when she tried to separate them, but when we refused to buy them he got quite agitated. We left, wondering whether he had a mental problem.

A mini-van share-taxi took us to Homs where we caught a jolly little bus to Aleppo, two and a half hours away. Yellow frayed curtains hung down over the top of the windscreen. A TV video showed lots of people dancing (badly, it seemed) while Arabic music blared loudly through the PA system. The video seemed to be just a film of a private function—there was nothing but dancing for the entire duration.

Half a dozen soldiers, unarmed, were jammed into the front of the bus. I pulled out a novel and read until we were almost into Aleppo.

The hotel was not easy to find. When at last we did we weren't much impressed, but took it anyway.

Darkness was falling and we went out into the streets. There were shops, workshops, souks, all busy. Here was a line of shoe-repairers, each with a heavy treadle sewing machine. There was a line of butchers with carcasses suspended from hooks. A shoddy, old-fashioned but fairly clean look was general. People were friendly—several times we were offered help to find our way.

We found a hotel that was better than we had, so arranged to go there in the morning. The manager also offered tours, useful in this area.

With falafels, bread and bananas we returned to our room. The very friendly, helpful and slightly simple hotel boy knocked on our door. He brought glasses of hot tea on a tray and, overcome with pleasure, kissed us on both cheeks.

It wasn't far to walk to the new hotel in the morning. The room wasn't ready, but Sheri had a look and declared it good, with a large balcony and bathroom, and hot-water radiators. Aleppo was still fairly cold, so the heating was welcome.

Soon after ten we set off on our tour in a small, under-powered yellow taxi, made in Iran. We drove north into the countryside, which was fairly stony-looking and not much populated. The taxi driver turned off the road onto a rough and rocky track leading to a building, but he was timid about his car's capability and stopped well before reaching it, leaving us to walk the rest of the way. In front of us was a ruined, isolated church, still standing except for its roof. But although about a thousand years old, it was not particularly interesting.

Two huge, shaggy brown puppies bounded playfully towards us. They were shepherds' dogs. We looked around for a while and went back to the car. As it picked its way cautiously down the hill the two parent dogs came racing after us. They were great, rangy beasts and I hoped they were as friendly as the pups. Somehow, I thought not.

We carried on to Saint Simeon's Basilica, where the famous old fellow had spent thirty-six years sitting on a pillar, preaching to a throng of devotees. He started on a three-metre pillar but had graduated to one eighteen metres tall by the time he died. A huge church was built around the pillar.

Today not much of the pillar is left, probably chipped away by souvenir hunters, but most of the church (minus roof) is still standing. Walking beside a wall for several hundred metres brings you to the Romanesque entrance, also still standing.

The day was cold and rainy and the ground had a covering of hailstones, which had fallen before our arrival. Light rain fell as we headed back to the taxi. We had to wait a while for the driver, who was reluctant to leave his tea and his friends in the little chai-house.

Now we drove south, painfully slowly at times. The driver would slip the car into neutral to save petrol—it might have been his lifeblood being dribbled away by the little engine!

The dead cities were our next destination. A little more than an hour later we arrived at Al-Bara, a rustic area where olive trees were plentiful in tilled fields, though the ground was very stony. The fields were very asymmetrical because of the rocky and uneven terrain. Derelict but historic walls and bushy areas contributed to this.

We came to a small pyramid and various ruined buildings. Two local lads showed us around these ancient places, but they were not the dead cities.We soon left to see the best-known of the abandoned cities of which we had read. They had not been on the day's itinerary, but being disappointed with what we had seen, except for Saint

Simeon's Basilica, we had agreed to pay extra to see this place.

We came to a hilly area, empty but for the abandoned buildings that rambled down a hillside. This was much better, an entire ruined town. Quite a bit of it was tumbled down, but a good many places were more or less intact, except of course for the roofs. Everything was built of large stone blocks, pillars and massive arches—the houses had been large. Probably the blocks were too big to be useful to later villagers and so had been left alone.

This area was open, with good views all around. Only a shepherd and his flock intruded on the scene, and they seemed natural to it. We spent an hour clambering about, discovering subterranean vaults that were probably for water, except one that looked like a family crypt. This was what we had come for.

Back in Aleppo we enjoyed our big, comfortable hotel room. Sheri washed clothes because we were here for two nights and the room and bathroom were each equipped with hot-water radiators, ideal for draping wet clothes. Then out into the wet night for dinner and an "Internet Coffee" as it was called, even though there was no coffee. But it was a good place to catch up on our emails.

On the way back Sheri bought little Syrian baklavas for coffee back in our room, using the trusty Birko, and by 10.30 we were comfortably re-ensconced.

At seven I woke after an unbroken sleep. Light rain was falling as I left Sheri asleep and went looking for breakfast.

Very few shops were open, not even the two tiny "supermarkets" at the bottom of the lane. So I returned to find Sheri just awake. We put Birko to use and had sweet pastries bought last night. Off we went to the National Museum, something of a shambles under renovation, but the exhibits went back six thousand years and were outstanding.

It was only fifteen or twenty minute's walk to the huge eleventh-century citadel, standing on a high mound, that was my only memory of my early visit to Aleppo. It compared to the Krak, but was far more ruinous inside. Neither was it anywhere near as massively built, though still impressive.

We entered the huge old souk, a labyrinth of vaulted alleys, colourfully lit with great brass chandeliers in the early main sections. There were plenty of tourist shops, but the farther sections were for locals, with many animal carcasses on extravagant display. These were meant to show the skill of the butchers. Of course all the usual items of daily life were for sale too—plastic buckets, shoes and so on.

We went into the great mosque. Sheri was obliged to wear a robe with a hood, one of many kept available, even though she had a head scarf. It was standard treatment for westerners, with a fifty lira fee, (one dollar) though entry was free.

Huge as it was, the mosque was more or less uniform inside, with nothing to vary the general appearance. Not for Islam the gaudy statues of the Orthodox Catholic church.

We tramped back through the muddy streets. Crossing the roads was always a bit of an adventure, though the drivers were not as aggressive as the Lebanese. After being on our feet for six or seven hours it was good to get back to the hotel. We had books to read, including a couple I found in the foyer. Later we went again into the still-rainy streets, visited the same internet café as last night, and had a good dinner.

Next day was predicted to be cold and wet and it was—a good day to leave. My bed-bug bites from Yemen had finally lost their itch. And now Sheri and I could both climb up the endless steep flights of castle steps quite easily. We had become fitter and healthier.

We caught a cab to the bus depot and by 9.15 were on the way to Homs, where we had changed buses on the way from the Krak. We had to wait three hours for the bus to Palmyra, our next stop, but sat comfortably in a sort of restaurant in the big bus depot building. We read books and the time passed easily. We commented on the fact that we saw pairs of Japanese girls travelling, but no boys. By 2.15 we were on our way.

The countryside down to Homs was fairly boring. It was flattish, with green fields interspersed with brown, ploughed areas, but had no real features. Then it began to change, drying out. Fertile plain changed to barren. There was almost no traffic.

Settlements became scarcer, then few and sparse. They sometimes had domed mud huts nearby that may have been small silos. Even these places gradually thinned down to nothing more than occasional tents, one of which had a satellite dish.

There were high, fairly rugged hills on the horizon on both sides of the road. I guessed we would enter these. We did, but Palmyra itself came as a surprise. Substantial three-storey houses, palms and trees lined the road, with plenty of cars driving on its cold, wet surface.

The bus stopped and disgorged its passengers. We ignored a fat fellow touting for hotel business and collected a scruffy cab to get to the Hotel Ishtar. After splashing through puddles for two or three kilometres, we were there. The driver took his agreed fifty lira, about one dollar.

The room was small, but the bed was huge. No TV, but a good reverse-cycle air con for heating. The bathroom was small but clean. There were clean towels, foot towels and shampoo. The bed had decent sheets and the room would be quiet since it looked over a back yard with a big palm tree in the middle.

"How much?" I asked the desk clerk.

"Twenty-five dollars, " was the answer.

"You have thirty per cent discount, right?" (Lonely Planet info.)

"No, but you can have it for twenty dollars."

"Fine, we'll take it."

And that was a fairly typical procedure for taking a hotel.

It was low season and we seemed the only customers. We settled in and went out for a walk. The few streets close by appeared solidly tourist-oriented, but everything further away was already closed for the evening. Sheri got lucky and found rolls of slide film, only slightly out of date.

At a well-lit restaurant, owned by a cousin of the hotel manager, (it was a small town) we went into a warm, cosy, tapestry-walled room. Very bright and cheerful it was. We had soup entrees, a delicious Bedouin-style lamb casserole with rice, a beer, teas and little sweets— all for ten dollars. And that was probably a tourist price!

The owner offered us a "Bedouin Experience" for the next evening. We would be driven to a tent where we would be fed and music would be played. It would be the closest we would get to an authentic experience, (and it would beat the stuffing out of staying in the hotel room all evening) so we agreed to go.

It was 8.30 when I woke, having got up twice in the night to bump up the temperature on the air-con. The bed was six feet wide but there was only one blanket and it was a bit too short to cover our shoulders properly. We went down to breakfast and found two places already laid for us. We ate up and headed out on foot to see what we'd come for—the ruins.

They were vast. Much of it was levelled, yet a lot remained standing. The main features were huge buildings surrounded by enormous pillars which would once have provided a kind of verandah all round when roofed.

Tour buses came, full of Iraqis and others. A couple of old buses disgorged a horde of schoolchildren, immediately pounced on by men offering camel rides. The usual variety of vendors tried to entice buyers, but nobody was too insistent.

Mostly, Syrians would take "no" for an answer. It all made for a lively scene, despite the keen, cold wind. At least the day was dry.

We found plenty to keep us busy for about three hours. The camera batteries had conked out and I bought new ones while Sheri walked back to the hotel—she was showings signs of a cold. I followed a little later.

At two o'clock there was a tour of some of the old tower tombs. We had to buy tickets from the museum, then find transport to the tombs. This was easy. One fellow had a bright-red 1957 Landrover which he had restored in a peculiarly Arab way, but he'd kept it more or less plain. I liked the vehicle, so we chose him.

It turned out that he also carried the man from the museum whose job it was to carry the enormous keys to unlock two of the many tombs, most of which were scattered up a barren valley. We were the first to arrive at one of these, a narrow, stone structure four stories high. On each level were rows of stone niches, two hundred and eighty in all. Strong draughts roared through the narrow, stone windows shaped like archers' slits. Probably their function had been to dry out the bodies.

The second tomb was underground and in much better condition. Part of it still had frescoes and ceiling ornamentation as well as statues. The influence was Greek, as we'd seen elsewhere here. Most of Palmyra dated back to around 200 AD, with a history of husband-killing Queen Zenobia, who later had Roman protection.

Being the first to enter the tomb was lucky because plenty of people followed us, including a tour bus load. Our driver took us back in the red Landrover and we agreed to have him pick us up tomorrow to take us to the bus station en route to Damascus.

At seven in the evening we were on the way to our "Bedouin experience", the only passengers in a short, high old bus. The driver told us it was a 1951 Mercedes and had been owned by his father and his grandfather before him. Now *that's* durability!

We reached a large Bedouin tent, several kilometres past the ruins. Inside there were rugs on the floor, cushions and low tables around the sides, and a large wood-heater. We sat around it, grateful for the warmth, along with a few Bedouin men.

An array of cold appetisers was put before us. Musicians began to warm up—men in black robes and youths in brown, with crossed bandoliers. At this stage we were still the only guests. Our driver sat beside us and told us what a good man and general benefactor Saddam Hussein had been. It wasn't the only time we heard this.

"I had pictures of him on my bus but I had to take them off. I was told tourists might not like them," he said. He was a sweet man …

The serious food came, a very large platter of chicken, meat that was perhaps camel, rice and vegetables. The musicians began to play and a busload of Syrian tourists arrived. Now there was dancing as well as music. One man, who seemed to have the status of a visiting celebrity, played a double pipe, breathing in through his nose as he played so that the sound never stopped. His cheeks and neck muscles worked like a bellows.

The Syrian guests were very lively and danced enthusiastically. It was a jolly evening, though we were glad to leave by eleven pm. We were due to leave in the morning and Sheri still seemed to have a bit of a cold. That hadn't stopped her dancing with the main singer, a huge man with a great belly under his black robe. He danced with the other guests too. It was part of his job to keep things moving and he did it well.

The bus for Damascus stopped at a petrol station next to a few shops, some distance from Palmyra. While we waited a boy asked us for a pen, then one for his father and another boy. Sheri obliged because she still had plenty from Yemen. The boy came back and playfully wanted more, but he was becoming a pest by the time we got on the bus.

We could only get the back seat and it was a hot journey. The Syrians seemed to like the air-con set that way.

Close to three hours later we pulled in at the Damascus bus terminal. We knew the taxis in to the city overcharged from here, but the fellow who accosted us wanted four hundred lira, double the normal exorbitant rate. He agreed to take two hundred. Of course when we got to the hotel he wanted two hundred *each*. I got change of a thousand lira note from the hotel and paid him just two hundred, leaving him complaining in the street.

The hotel, however, was full. We ended up at a nearby one catering to locals, with no customers. It was much cheaper at $20, but not so different from what we could have got for $30. Or so we thought.

Sheri was feeling reasonably good, despite her sore throat. She did some hand washing and we used the air-con to heat up the room to dry it off. Then we went out and found that the temperature had dropped.

At the hotel that we'd first tried we made a booking for the next day—the current one was really too bleak. For the next several hours we cruised around shopping, finding an internet café and having dinner. Sheri succeeded in booking a hotel in Amman, Jordan, by email. We expected to arrive there late in the day and it would be easier to have a booking.

Back at the hotel the desk staff had turned off our air-con by a remote switch and the room was cold. Bastards! All in all it was a fairly drab day. But we had a TV and watched "On the Ropes" with Meg Ryan.

Next day we trundled our rucksacks around to the Sultan Hotel, a much better place. The old city was very close, but the first stop was the museum in the opposite direction. Plenty of interest there, including statues and sarcophagi in the big garden, where there was also a coffee shop with a lot of character. Sheri went on to look in handicraft shops while I went on to the adjacent military museum, costing just a few cents to enter.

Mostly it had swords—individual swords, clusters of swords, piles of swords—hundreds of the things. Most of them looked ancient and valuable, with curved ones being the most common. Pistols were the next most numerous items, from flintlocks to Colt 45's, tiny to huge. Again, hundreds.

Funky old planes sat outside, next to an old mosque. A lot of pre-1945 artillery was left over from the French occupation and from failed attempts to suppress local revolution against that occupation, or so I read.

Back to the hotel for a break and a coffee, feet up with a book. Then to the old city, the not-so-interesting long, covered souk, the huge Ummayad mosque, high, enormous and impressive in its architecture. Sheri bought a few souvenirs and in the evening we went to quite a swanky restaurant for dinner, partly from lack of choice!

We were out early next morning to grab a cab to Baramanka Garage. It was the bus station for Amman, but also the place where you could catch a huge, old, yellow American taxi. Double the bus price but faster, they went all through the day, not just at seven a.m..

The local cab driver tried to get us to take one of his friends' non-shared taxis to Amman at an exorbitant cost. No deal. Then we were approached by someone offering a bus. This turned out to be genuine—a new company with a magnificent, brand-new Mitsubishi coach, leaving shortly. Perfect!

We sat aboard the bus, looking at one of the big yellow service taxis. The driver was loading the roof rack higher and higher with all sorts of baggage. The car would be full of locals, some of whom would smoke cigarettes all the way with the windows shut. We hadn't missed out on much …

JORDAN

Getting across the border was a slow process, mainly because the visa office was unattended. Nobody else needed one, so it was just us infidels who kept the bus waiting. Even so, we were in Amman barely four hours after leaving Damascus, although the guide book gave the normal time as seven hours.

The Palace Hotel it did not live up to its name and cost more than we were used to. Was this a sign of things to come in Jordan?

We arranged to hire a car for a week. The manager sent a driver to take us to his office, a big, handsome fellow who drove very fast. The manager was a good-natured man and gave us his views on Iraqis, chiefly to the effect that they were very difficult people who needed a strong leader to keep them in order. Another nod of approval for Sadam …

Around seven we went out for dinner. Arab streets look better by night. You don't see so much of the dirt and the bright shop lights reflect off the multi-coloured merchandise, which is often on open display in stalls.

We couldn't find any restaurants for a while, but eventually located a scruffy joint specializing in barbecued chickens. We went upstairs, where the ceiling was so low I couldn't stand up straight. But it was brightly lit and a young woman was sharing a table with her little girl. She translated for us with the waiter, so we got chicken, rice and "fettush", the salad. Not too bad.

Back on the street, dodging cars, I bought a can of cold beer (the restaurants did not serve alcohol, but some shops here sold it) and Sheri bought some local biscuits. The young punk behind the counter was quite rude, but that was unusual.

Back in our hotel room the hot-water radiator was off. We needed it, so I went down to the desk. The attendants told me they had a routine of switching the heat on and off at intervals to save money. This again! They turned it back on, so I returned to my stubby of beer and watched "CSI" on Dubai One.

Sheri slept until eight, though I woke early. The water was hot, unlike last night, and we were able to shower.

We knew there wasn't a lot to see in Amman, but we had a day to spend. So we located the remains of an Ummayad mosque not far from the hotel, where a scruffy cat mewed half-savagely, half-piteously for food.

A long road climbed up to a more salubrious area than the scruffy "downtown". We passed the Turkish Embassy, guarded by a bored-stupid soldier with a bullet-proof vest and automatic rifle.

Sheri was looking for some handicraft shops. The best of these was genuinely interesting with quite a lot of antique wares— wooden bowls, tall brass teapots with long spouts, and pottery. Prices were high, however.

The long walk up had been good exercise, but Sheri was still feeling the effects of her sore throat and the cold, rather smoggy air was aggravating that. We found a good quality supermarket of the kind that expats use and stocked up for tomorrow's car trip.

When we got back to the hotel we took it easy, read a bit, had a beer and ate a *schwarma*, the local version of a souvlaki. The weather was supposed to improve tomorrow and, best of all, we'd have our own transport. That should make for a better time than a drab Amman hotel, too stingy to keep the place heated!

The Jerusalem restaurant, one of the few around, was recommended by Lonely Planet with the reservation that the staff were grumpy. But it was the besuited manager himself who confronted us with "Do you speak Arabic?" in a hostile tone that sounded like a challenge.

"No," I replied, giving him a big smile, "But I see you speak English."

That seemed to disarm him. The menu was only in Arabic, but the manager described a dish. He named a price that seemed high and when I paid the bill he was reluctant to give change.

Never mind, the food was good even if the service was bad. For one like him there were many who were hospitable. We were reminded of that when we bought some sweet confections and were kindly assisted.

The alarm went off at 6.45, though I'd woken an hour earlier with a dose of Sheri's sore throat. Some water and a few sips of whiskey helped. We showered and packed, then went down to breakfast, where a man from the car- hire firm was already waiting.. He took us back to the office to pick up our Peugeot 307.

Fortunately there wasn't much traffic in this area and I didn't have any problem driving the left hand drive car, except for flicking on the windscreen wipers instead of the indicators. We missed our way and had to stop to get directions, but soon after that we were leaving Amman on the way to Jerash.

The hills were green and we began to see the comparison with Tuscany mentioned by the guide book. The presence of quite a few trees helped with that impression, though it was more noticeable later heading west from Jerash towards the Dead Sea.

The Jerash Roman ruins were extensive, but what was surprising was the re-creation of Roman troop tactics, gladiator fights and chariot races in the ancient hippodrome. We hadn't been interested when asked to buy tickets outside, expecting nothing better than some corny capering from some locals dressed up as gladiators. But when Sheri jokingly offered them half price and it was accepted, we found ourselves inside.

The only other spectators were in a Japanese tour group. They didn't have an interpreter, just an Arabic-only speaking guide, but he made it clear to the Swedish manager that they were in a hurry. Then the compere, a young Jordanian clad in Roman-style armour, announced in amazingly stentorian tones, and in perfect Oxford English, exactly what was happening at each step.

It was instructive as well as entertaining. The well-drilled troops showed various fighting strategies, including a wedge-shaped tortoise formation using shields that let an engineer work to open a gate under cover. Gladiators, who we were told used to be drawn from the scum of the prisons, showed their fighting styles. A beefy lot they were, too. At the close, the Swedish man said to me that they had cut short the chariot race because of the tour group. But, as compensation, would I like a circuit on one of the chariots? "We aren't insured…" he tailed off.

It sounded a good idea to me and I climbed aboard the little chariot, keeping my knees bent and loose while I gripped the edge of the top with both hands. When the horses were urged to the gallop the ride felt violently powerful, especially rounding the tight turns at the ends of the hippodrome. Great fun!

The car pointed west, heading for the Dead Sea. The roads were fairly minor, and sometimes rough. But the driving was easy enough and the Peugeot had good suspension. We had to get back on the freeway to Amman before turning off to Madabar, a much prettier place and one where tourists prefer to stay.

We looked at a couple of hotels, then tried the expensive Madabar Inn. We took a look at a room, found it very good indeed, and asked for discount. We took it at US$60, a bargain by comparison with the places we'd been staying. We felt the need to boost our morale after the grey days and grey city of Amman, and a string of hotels that were always frustrating in one way or another.

However, even here there was a problem—there was plenty of hot water, but no cold. Thus, no usable showers and no toilet refills. It took about three hours to fix the problem, which turned out to be hotel-wide. “Ten minutes, ten minutes,” was the cry, but it was a lie. At last the water came through and Sheri could shower and wash her hair. We had dinner at a quite expensive restaurant. Might as well preserve the style!

It was nice to wake up in a good hotel after an unbroken night’s sleep. The curtains pulled back to give a really great view over the town and valley. Not far away was the church of St. George, which had woken me pleasantly with the sound of its bells, a rapid-fire pealing. At breakfast we were the only guests; all the others were on tours—long gone, poor sufferers.

Towards ten we ambled off on a quiet little road. It was mountainous and at a certain point we stopped at Mt. Nebo, where a church was a shrine to Moses. This, it is still believed, was where God showed him the Promised Land, and a fine view it was. The ancient church was more or less in ruins, but they were very well preserved, enclosed under a sort of modern shed. The mosaics of the floors and walls were beautiful, some restored. It seemed the Franciscan friars responsible for its maintenance still used it as a church. It was simple, unpretentious and yet impressive, having an air of serenity in spite of its galvanized iron shelter.

The little car dropped down to the Dead Sea. Now the road ran along the base of a fringe of hills, leaving the low, bare cliffs that fell away to the water. Through the misty air we could discern similar hills far away on the other side.

We came to organized swimming beaches, so we picked one. The coast was too rugged to pull over and swim just anywhere, and we'd need a fresh-water shower after swimming in the intensely salty water.

It was a warm day, far different from further north. We plonked our gear under some shade and paid for a plastic table and chairs.

You really did float like a cork in this water. It was even hard to keep our feet on the bottom because our legs tended to float up. When we swam our feet were in the air. The water, incidentally, tasted terrible.

There were lots of visitors, mainly Arabic. Most of the women did not swim and made no clothing concession to the warm environment. The foreigners, on the other hand, tended to stay close to the water in their bikinis. One ridiculously-muscular man, probably American, strutted along covered in black mud. He looked like the Incredible Hulk.

We had agreed to look after the gear of a young English family while they swam. When they returned after an hour or two, we left. Sheri drove, with me nagging her to keep the inside wheels on the road. That made a change from her nagging me to go slowly. We turned inland and climbed up to Karak, the site of a crusader castle. The hotel we took was pretty basic, but the choice seemed poor.

The restaurant next door was expensive, but when we said something to the owner he replied: "OK, no tax, no service charge." So we left a decent tip. As we were leaving he insisted on giving us ginger tea. I found it delicious. Sheri got a good coffee.

Back in our hotel room, two young Aussie girls knocked on our door. They were studying Arabic in Amman and were finding university life there very isolated and cloistered. So they'd cleared off together for a weekend away. They talked for over an hour, glad to talk to fellow Aussies. We wondered if they would see out their year, especially when one said she was "considering her options."

It had been four weeks since we left Adelaide. We took leave of our shy, kindly landlord and cruised around Karak Castle for an hour before pushing on. Really, its history was more interesting than its structure. The principal crusader, Reynald de Chantillon, had been something of a pirate. He'd had a small fleet of boats built, transported by camel to the Dead Sea, re-assembled, then used to raid cities on the far shore. In the end Saladin defeated him by siege, let his men go and chopped off his head. Sounded fair enough to me.

We travelled slowly by the King's Highway through the mountains before emerging onto the Desert Highway. Even here the road was a bit choppy, but good for an easy 130 kph most of the time. Big 4wd's whizzed past us occasionally, going at least 160.

After a couple of hours we turned off for Wadi Rum. For some time the flat desert had given way to powerful rock formations and these were very evident as we drove fifteen kilometres along a side road to reach the elaborate Visitors' Centre.

We could see the huge Seven Pillars of Wisdom rock, namesake of T.E. Lawrence's book. I had not known about the origin of the name before, although the book was one of my favourites. We booked a five-hour 4WD tour for the following day, through a smart-alec twenty-year-old with a silly hat. There was nowhere to stay here so we left for Aqaba, on the coast of the Red Sea, about an hour away.

Aqaba was a surprise. It was busy, bustling, full of resorts and tall buildings. It was a lot more pleasant than Amman. The foreshore was lined with palm trees and the promenade was bordered by showy shops. The narrow, sandy beach was solid with restaurants and concessions offering chairs and tables. In the darkening evening some people were still swimming, though the women limited themselves to sitting in the shallows on their white plastic chairs, ankles in the water.

We found an internet café. I bought a can of beer and we had a satisfying meal on the balcony of a nearby restaurant. Sheri hand-washed some clothes, which we hung to dry on our balcony. Such things were our little routine. At local shops we bought provisions, ready for our 4wd trip tomorrow.

Next morning a change of weather greeted us, with light rain. It was fairly forbidding as we left, but tailed off as we approached Wadi Rum.

There we were directed to a decrepit 4wd with a cracked and filthy windscreen. There were plenty of other vehicles there, so I refused the old bomb and chose a good one. I didn't know what their system was. It didn't matter as long as we got co-operation, which we did.

Our driver owned his car, a '91 Nissan Patrol, still okay after nearly half a million kilometres. He was a tall man, around thirty-five years old, and spoke good English which he'd learned on the job. His name, Antik, sounded hard to pronounce. "Just think of "antique"," he said. Good enough.

The weather was now warm and fine, if misty. Giant rock structures reared hundreds of metres from the desert floor. They were fantastically shaped by erosion. Much of that, Antik explained, was actually water erosion from the time when the sea had covered this land. That looked credible: the scalloping and ribbing reminded me of water-cut rock.

We saw Lawrence's spring and the remains of the house where he had lived for a while. That consisted of a stone-block wall built by the early Naboteans well over two thousand years ago. It was close to a wave-cut overhanging rock and would not have needed much of a roof.

I was interested in the performance of the car through the soft sand, so Antik let me drive. The diesel motor lugged us steadily through the sand, only the deeper parts requiring 4wd. At one point Sheri and I climbed a steep dune for the view, and hard work that was, for we slipped back two steps for every three. At another place, a natural rock bridge, we clambered up the rock to the top, also not easy. Sheri asked the driver if anyone ever fell. “Yes!” he said. He went on to say that a Chinese man had come down the wrong way, taken a tumble, and finished up in hospital.

There was an odd plant-top lying on the sandy ground. Antik said they grew down into the sand. His brother had stomach ulcers and collected them—the ground-up root was therapeutic. Antik said he’d find one. “Looks like a dick!” he said to me. Soon he returned with one. I couldn’t see much resemblance, but who knows …

The wind blew up, stronger and stronger. Light-coloured sand began whipping across in gusts. As the wind strengthened the heavier red sand also began blowing, rattling harshly against the windows. Luckily I’d opted for a proper, closed vehicle instead of benches in the back of a utility, because you really knew it if the sand hit you in the face before you got the window up.

The temperature dropped and the sand gusts began to obscure the view. We were glad enough to finish our four-and-a-half-hour trip. Other people, less lucky, were just setting out, scarf-wrapped to the eyes, in the backs of open utes. They would have a bit of an ordeal.

We left for Petra, about ninety minutes away. There we found a three-star hotel, freshly re-furbished. Sometimes you get lucky! So we had a large, luxurious room and ensuite, with good views from the balcony. Never mind the toilet that flushed ineffectually, (normal enough in this region) and clear signs of salt damp in walls. No blessings are unqualified in third-world countries—you have to focus on the positive, unless the negative is too awful to bear.

A clear, bright morning arrived. A couple of kilometres down the road, through the little town, we came to the entrance of the famous remains of Petra. A two-day pass cost us $52. Very quickly there were offers of donkeys and camels to ride the 1.2 kilometre distance through the narrow ravine that enters ancient Petra. But, like most people, we preferred to walk, wondering at the towering, smooth-worn cliffs overhanging the narrow roadway.

We popped out of the ravine to stare in amazement at the huge, carved tomb that confronted us across a sandy, arena-like space. The abruptness of this made us gasp in surprise. The scene was lively: tourists, dark-faced boys on trotting donkeys, stalls selling trinkets, pacing camels, all dwarfed by the enormous pinky-red temple carved into the cliff. It was like a re-creation of a time past. That impression stayed with me elsewhere in Petra throughout the day. In that sense the city is not dead at all—this is the new life it has found.

To put the place in perspective, Petra is a giant, jagged amphitheatre of high, rocky hills around a winding river valley. Two long, major cliff faces are honeycombed with tombs and temples, but many others have been dug in any possible area. Some of the temples are huge. Nearly all are excavated and sculpted, with only a few using some building blocks, though one of the largest is entirely built of blocks.

Once you take in the scale of the place, what strike you are the incredibly variegated colours of the tomb ceilings. It's like abstract art, but natural. The sedimentary rocks are blue, red, yellow and black. The colours are vivid, not dull. If you rub the yellow rock with your finger it comes off on your skin, but the other striata are harder. These striated bands are everywhere—the slightest erosion reveals them and they are not faded inside the tombs and temples.

We walked, climbed and exhausted ourselves. After a lunch from our day bag we took donkeys for the eight hundred steps to the place called The Monastery. The way was a narrow path with frequent sets of steps cut. Sheri's donkey got on with the job, but mine was reluctant and often seemed to stagger on the very edge. I just relaxed and let the animal make the climb I was sure it knew well. Besides, the drop was not far enough to seem fatal, a consolation to me!

The Monastery was a truly enormous temple, cut out of the rock, high up away form the valley. The colour was only brown—the variegated rock was absent here. A short distance away was a sacrificial area, overlooking valleys that fell far away to Palestine.

It was a weary walk back out of Petra and we were bushed at the end of it. We'd walked and climbed the whole day. In the long entry-ravine, horse-drawn carts rattled through at full speed, seeking to make as many trips as possible now that everybody was leaving. The sounds echoed from the high walls.

At six a.m. we got someone else's wake-up call, but slept on till eight. There was no rush today. By ten we were back at ancient Petra—there was still quite a bit we hadn't seen.

Again we did a lot of climbing, but by one p.m. we were done.

The plan was to drive slowly back to Amman Airport, leave the car, and catch a late-night flight to Sharjah. We had time to kill. Eventually we rejoined the highway and noticed that plenty of other people drove slowly too, though others did the opposite.

The fuel economy meter on the car dropped to a steady 6.2 litres per hundred, a good thing because we didn't want to refill the tank. We had only a few dinars left for the airport and weren't due to leave until 2.30 next morning. We'd need a coffee or two in the meantime.

We found Car Park Three near Terminal 2, as arranged, and five minutes later someone arrived to collect the car, sharp at 7.30. It was good to go inside the warm terminal—the temperature outside was only twelve degrees. We found a café and settled down to pass the time. At last, after delays, numerous baggage x-rays and body checks, emigration procedures and so on, we boarded the plane and taxied out promptly at 2.30.

Air Arabia has a new fleet of A-320's, nice planes, one class. Sheri and I had three seats to ourselves. When the plane had reached its cruising altitude and the seatbelt sign went off, I went to the back and found several empty rows of seats. Rolling up a pullover for a pillow, I curled up and went to sleep, leaving Sheri to do the same.

At 5 a.m. Jordan time, 7 a.m. Sharjah time, we landed in daylight. There was an hour's transit time before we flew to Muscat, capital of Oman, a short flight away.

OMAN

Leaving Muscat airport we were struck by the surroundings: expensive, well-maintained, built and landscaped to impress, like Dubai. The taxi, plush and new like the whole fleet of airport cabs, pulled up near the fish market on the Mutrah Corniche. We'd say 'coastal road', but 'corniche' has a lot more class!

We tried one recommended hotel but it was overpriced. The second was okay, but the room was small. The third was cheapest of all and the room was big. A brassy-looking, dyed-blonde woman in the foyer looked like a prostitute. Hmmm. What sort of hotel was this? We took the room anyway; we'd leave next day if we found a problem.

We fell asleep for a couple of hours, then reluctantly got up and went out. The local ATM's wouldn't work so I went back to the hotel desk for the passports so that I could use a bank. The hotel clerk gave me one but wanted to keep the other.

"You have not paid yet," he said.

"What kind of hotel wants to be paid when people arrive?" I answered, though I had my suspicions.

"I keep one passport," he insisted.

"You have no right to keep passports. Hand it over."

Reluctantly he did, but took photocopies. Later, when I had some money, I paid him for one night. "So you will not be afraid," I teased, laughing. Good-natured joking always seemed to smooth out a situation with Arab men.

The esplanade was quite beautiful, especially as we left the built-up area. The little harbour was full with shipping , including two cruise liners. Tourists were numerous on the streets, which had plenty of pavement cafes and restaurants. The Lonely Planet said tourism was suffering in Oman, but it didn't look that way.

Later the evening air was warm. Rugged mountains ran down close to the sea and we had dinner on the street, where the views were glorious.

Back at the hotel we saw a hard-looking Yemeni woman in a room close to ours. She had earlier helped us with a TV problem and was an obliging person. Lady of the night with a heart of gold? Still, I took the phone off the hook, in case of misplaced midnight calls.

But apart from some loud hallway conversations in the night, involving the Yemeni woman and what may have been customers, we were not disturbed. It was nine o'clock when we woke up, though of course only seven by our Jordanian body clocks. We both felt spaced out. Breakfast was minimal, just some of our own food in the hotel room. We tidied up, sat down and did a bit of trip planning.

Just after lunch on the esplanade we caught a cab to the CBD in Ruwi, one of the three major districts of Muscat—Mutrah, where we were, was another. But things were shut until four p.m. so we passed the time drinking Pepsis in an air-conditioned KFC. Even in this season Muscat was already warm. In summer it would be very hot.

At four we bought plane tickets to Salalah, a thousand kilometres away across the desert in the south. The idea was to spend a few days there before returning to Muscat. We hadn't been able to get a flight later in the week so we had to do things in reverse.

In a Kodak shop we were able to buy a couple more rolls of slide film, though it took a while. It's pretty much obsolete, of course. But all over the shop we could hear the words "slide film" in the middle of Hindi sentences, so they were onto it. After twenty minutes we had the film.

Another cab took us to old Muscat. Like everything we'd seen here it was immaculate. A lot of money had been spent: the CBD was new and stylish, the corniche was beautifully established. Infrastructure and landscaping everywhere was at least at Adelaide standard, yet Oman is not oil-rich.

In old Muscat we saw enough to know it was worth returning, but now it was dark. We took a taxi back to the hotel.

Later, at the same restaurant as last night, we watched a group of Omani boys. Freshly released from study, clustered round their tables, they were well dressed in robes and Omani caps. Each had his little perfume tassel hanging down one side just below his neck, an oddly effeminate touch to my eyes, but normal for Arab male dress here. Almost all wore glasses, even though they were only around thirteen years old. But, like boys anywhere, they were playful and cheeky, making the waiter grumpy.

The souk was nearby, a long alley, roofed over in decorated wood. Sheri was keen to have a look, so I went along. At the other end we bought a few provisions. Now Sheri wanted to check the internet, but I was feeling lazy, so left her and slowly strolled along the seaward side of the esplanade. Light rippled off the water and little groups of people and families lingered, chatting quietly. Out in the harbour a magnificent dhow gleamed faintly. I had seen it shining golden in the daylight, a thing of varnished glory, no doubt a wealthy man's pride.

We were up early to catch the plane, a simpler routine than usual because it was a domestic flight. Through the cabin windows we could see brown, mountainous land, like so much of Arabia.

Salalah was a small place. Scruffily sub-tropical, lots of palm trees within a couple of kilometres of the white sandy beach, multi-storey buildings going up in isolation in broad, empty, dusty places as you moved inland. It looked like a pleasant little fishing town trying to grow into a Muscat-style city, but with a long way to go.

Our hotel was one of these new buildings, with a quite elaborate facade. The Indian manager was friendly, the room was large and nicely furnished, yet it was cheap. Salalah just couldn't be much in demand. Even car hire was cheap. The courteous, well-spoken Omani agent brought a new Nissan Tiida round to the hotel for us.

We took a drive to the beach. It was broad and clean, with good-sized waves tumbling in. Tomorrow we'd take a trip along the coast.

In the morning the car headed west toward Yemen, not far away. We passed a large container-handling port before reaching open terrain. Now the road led inland to high country, where we came to Job's tomb.

This was in a small, unprepossessing building guarded by an agitated old man. He did not like the pile of shoes people had respectfully left outside and angrily swept them off the step.

Inside there was a three-metre long rectangle covered in rich cloth. The old man had left frankincense on the charcoal burner, but we could see the offerings tray nearby. He seemed to be doing pretty well.

Was it really Job's tomb? I'm pretty skeptical about these things, but it's true that time here, in these old and arid regions, just isn't the same as in the West. Some things move very slowly or, seemingly, not at all

The guide book recommended the tomb for the views alone, but the day was hazy. We got back in the car and left for a place called Maghsayel.

The road was steep and mountainous with many gorges cut through the rock. Maghsayel was a long, broad beach peppered by red, octagonal beach shelters and palm trees. Good, actually. But each concrete shelter was occupied, if not by people, then by their picnic things. Besides, there was nothing to sit on.

We carried on to the promontory at the end. This was known for the blowholes on the limestone ledges above the sea, but the tide was too low, though even the whoosh of wind through the holes was a bit scary. A full spout of water from the bigger holes would be dangerous.

The area was well fenced for hundreds of metres with expensive stainless- steel wire, four thick strands of it, topped with glossy, sealed hardwood timber. It made Aussie permapine fencing look pretty basic.

We walked along the rocky shore, disturbing dozens of large black crabs, before driving back to a beachside restaurant. The air was very warm and humid, but the breeze was strong.

After lunch we pushed further, climbing into the mountains. Yemen was perhaps a hundred kilometres away. This terrain was empty; the stony mountains seemed not to be populated, except by a soldier's checkpoint. The sense of isolation grew as we went on—it felt like no-man's-land. There was no point in persevering, so we turned around.

Back in Salalah we drove past dozens of palm trees with smaller banana palms among them. Nearby were the partly-excavated ruins of the ancient port of Zafar, visited by Ibn Battuta. I was mostly interested in a well-preserved boat lying outside.

About eight metres long, it came to a slender point at both ends. It had been propelled by five oars each side, probably with one man to each oar. What intrigued me was its construction. It was made of wood, but sewn together with lashings. It was intricately done and even now everything was rock-solid. It was different from the outriggers of Goa, in India, because it had been given an extended chine coming out from each side to give it beam and therefore stability, which stopped it being a mere canoe.

All this required very skilful scarfing and stitching, the whole boat being sealed with a hard, gum-based waterproof layer. The craftsmanship was wonderful.

Next stop was the souk, where Sheri bought a couple of frankincense burners and two bags of the fragrant resin. This was where it all came from and there were vast quantities on display at many stalls. In another area were barber shops—my hair and beard were well due for a cut.

The haircut was normal, but the beard trim was so short that the reflection of my face gave me a fright! I hadn't seen my upper lip in twenty-five years, and then only briefly. But it was the facial and other treatment to follow that was exceptional. The barber ushered me into a side room where he scrubbed my face with something abrasive, like Solvol soap. A creamy massage followed, then a steam, then variations on the theme. All this was new to me and I got a glimmering of why the old crusaders didn't want to go home.

Sheri had been waiting for me all this time and now came into the shop. But I was enjoying the experience and had no intention of cutting things short. (the barber had already done that)

Last was a massage of the back of the head, neck, shoulders, backs of arms and each side of the spine. It was a strong, even painful experience, but it certainly felt good. All this cost five rials, about twenty dollars, and even if I was overcharged I didn't care.

At an Indian restaurant that evening the manager sat down and had a long chat. He'd been in Salalah for twenty eight years.

"Ten years ago," he said, "This was just a small town. Now it is a free port and many ships come in here. They unload to smaller ships that go all over the Arabian Gulf."

Now I knew for certain what all the container cranes were for, and why the town had such a rapidly-expanding look about it.

Back in the hotel an Omani man greeted us, shook my hand and made the Arab gesture of touching the right hand over the heart. I liked that. Men throughout the Arab countries greeted each other with a warm cameraderie, even strangers like me. There was an assumption of friendly understanding that seemed perfectly genuine and unreserved. They were always polite and respectful to Sheri, never sleazy.

The next day was a good one. We ran south along the coast to see the Khor Rouri ruins, a pre- Islamic port that was once the focus of trade as far as India in frankincense, bronze and iron. A local family had also come to look and we scrambled over the place more or less together.

Not far away was an utterly remote, beautiful beach which we reached by car over a bumpy track. We swam in clear water at a perfect temperature. Here you could swim naked in the Arabian Sea, with not so much as a distant shepherd to bother about. It was about as perfect as you could wish for.

Further south was the tomb of someone called Bin Ali, a small white building, again with a long, rectangular coffin in the middle, covered by a rich red cloth. A number of people walked very slowly and reverently around this, always in one direction. Presumably a local saint, he was certainly much respected.

Outside was a graveyard, a wasteland of stone. Nearly all the graves were roughly marked with an unshaped vertical slab, not very high, to mark it. Most carried no inscription. The graves were not in rows; it would be hard to pick one from another.

A few kilometres south was a coastal village. We turned off the main road to enter. It was bizarre picking our way through the narrow road, more like an alley, that threaded between the two-storied buildings. The village was almost certainly built in the days of donkeys and was not meant to provide a clear passage. Most of the houses were crumbling and abandoned, but not all. There was no-one to be seen.

Yet as we reached the sea there was a restaurant with a dozen or so cars scattered around, mostly expensive 4wd's. We went to the covered balcony on the top floor to have lunch. The tables were separated by lattice partitions to give privacy to family groups. There appeared to be several wives to one man, as befitted those who could afford the expensive vehicles outside, but only a few children. Perhaps other children were at home, being looked after by the junior wives.

Across the bay of the little fishing port was a green-domed mosque where it seemed all the local men were praying. An aged voice creaked out the same phrase over the loudspeaker, with minor variations, for a long time. Eventually there were choruses of replies. It was a Saturday and this was traditional, rural, Arabia. Did it beat a barbecue, beer and a footy match? Who's to say?

Behind us was a jetty with a long line of fibreglass fishing boats, all with outboard motors. Several men were cutting up fish on the stone seawall. Below them on the rocks a large shark lay dead.

At the seaward end, three large motorized dhows were moored. One was unloading a catch of large swordfish, the biggest of which had their bills cut off. In the stern of the boat, behind the wheelhouse and sitting in cushioned comfort, were two well-dressed men, plump and affluent-looking. I guessed one was the *nakhoda*, or skipper of the vessel, and the other was the owner.

Driving out of the little town we saw large, new houses. These were what people could afford now—it seemed no-one wanted the old places of stone and timber. The new houses would have nothing like the natural insulating capacity of the old, but now there was air-conditioning. The old houses were slowly falling to pieces here in this remote and beautiful place. Could this be the new France or Italy for Europeans wanting a rustic holiday home?

On the way back we tried to reach an area in the hills where we knew there would be greenery, pools and perhaps waterfalls. There was a "road closed" sign on a gravel track, but we scrambled up in the car until the wheels spun uselessly on the steep, rocky surface. So we turned around and went back. Further down the main road we came to a proper bitumen side-road, not the pot-holed track described in Lonely Planet.

This led us easily up into the hills until we reached a sort of very large picnic spot. There were many cars spread throughout, with groups of people sitting or standing. In one place a dozen camels clustered round a truck, being fed what looked like leafy braches.

There was water, but in this season it lay in still, brown rivers and pools. We'd had enough, so went back to Salalah and returned the car. It had been a long day.

At breakfast we met a New Zealand couple, expats working in Dubai. Around our age, they were quite chatty, though he was quieter and more reserved. She was short and blonde, he tall and lanky. They invited us to stay with them in Dubai when we returned to Sharjah, only half an hour away.

We caught the plane back to Muscat, where I'd arranged for a Toyota Prado to be waiting for us. It was almost brand-new and felt wonderful to drive on the road to Nizwa, a large town a couple of hundred kilometres inland from Muscat. We passed many small towns set among palm trees and silhouetted against high mountains.

Once we had to stop for an accident. Half the road was blocked by an overturned car, surrounded by people who'd stopped their cars to help, or maybe just to look. The victims seemed to be already out. An ambulance had passed us earlier, heading back to Muscat.

At Nizwa the first hotel we tried was full, but the second had a fine, large room. When we went out for dinner I couldn't work out the 4wd selection knob. Sheri saw a Toyota dealer, so we stopped to ask one of the people there. He advised me and I thought I had it figured out. However, when we got back to the hotel after dinner I got out the manual. It was literally rigid with mould, who knew why in a near-new car. I pried the pages open until I had the right section. Then I found the car was a permanent 4wd model and what the Toyota rep had told me was a load of rubbish, or maybe I hadn't understood him properly. Probably the latter.

The main idea in the morning was to take the sixteen kilometre climb up to Jebel Sham, a 3,000 metre-high mountain. Near the foot was Ghul, an abandoned village adjacent to a wadi. We drove a few hundred metres over the rough wadi shale to explore the little old town.

Just across the other side of the wadi, at a narrow point where it led between cliffs, a young goat bleated from a cranny fifty metres up the cliff- face. Somewhere below its mother called. Eventually, an old man came to look. He shook my hand, looked up at the kid and lifted his hands in a "what to do?" gesture.

Sheri and I walked through the green gardens that bordered the wadi. They had palm trees scattered through them and stone walls to protect them from the river.

We climbed up the steep, rocky path leading up through the village, poking curiously into the empty and mostly roofless houses. They were crudely built of loose, un-mortared stones with mud chinking. Most were two-storied, but the bottoms were adapted to the irregular, rocky slopes. Precision had been impossible, but the buildings seemed solid enough. The upper story floors were made of sawn palm-tree halves overlaid with palm canes about three to four centimeters wide. Mud was packed over that. It was a version of wattle and daub.

The whole rustic place was quite derelict, but the gardens at the bottom were still tended, presumably by the people who lived in the newer houses established on the other side of the wadi. We would see other examples that day of old-style buildings abandoned for new houses.

The Jebel Sham road was supposed to be very rough, but road-building was going on and a lot of bitumen road had been laid. This was a bit disappointing since we had the Prado to play with, but soon the road became so steep and twisting that I often had to drop back to first gear and rarely got beyond second. Then the bitumen ended and we were indeed on a narrow, steep, rough road. There were only a few other vehicles coming towards us, but in order to pass we had to pull over where possible and wait for the other driver to reach that point.

At last we reached the top, a dead end as we expected it might be, but lacking the view we'd hoped for. Sheri fed flat Arab bread to a hungry goat and we descended the mountain.

Back at Ghul, we tried to drive up the wadi. But the track wound very tightly through the newer houses, from which hurried women. They clutched little bits of woven wool to sell and were good-natured, but very persistent. One came running down the rocky path with a baby on her hip.

It was too much for us. Feeling wrenched at the poverty that must be driving these women and faced with the almost-impossible narrow, twisting track, we gave up and retreated.

Next stop was a place called Al Hamra. This was a very pretty town, with clear water flowing through channels by the roadway. Everywhere were gardens of palm trees and greenery, often enclosed by old mud walls.

As we went further into the little town, we saw three-storey mud-brick buildings on one side of the road. Poking around, we found that these had electricity connected to them in a very rough fashion, (wires through the windows) but were obviously abandoned. However, there were some signs of occupation. It seemed the big, old buildings were used by squatters.

Then, still on the same side higher side of the road, away from the gardens bordering the stream on the other side, we came to a large area of mud-brick houses straggling uphill. All were empty. Some had locks on the doors, but most stood in a state of partial collapse with rubbish on the floors. It was a little eerie to look on the evidence of past lives, just left behind.

Later in the afternoon we sought out a castle, really the palace of a local imam. Far from the town in open country, it had been built over a thirty-year period, finished in 1670 and last lived in around 1930. A lot of restoration had been done, but some rooms were original. Lonely Planet called it "whimsical".
Certainly it was hard to understand the layout.

One feature was a system of tunnel-like ducts and openings, which were a sort of air-conditioning system. From the high top were magnificent views all around of desert, adjoining palm groves, the far town and distant mountains.

There was supposed to be a hotel in a town called Bahla. People said they knew it and it was just "up there". When we got to that point someone else said it was somewhere else. After three such attempts we gave up. There were few hotels in this area, it seemed, and we ended by returning to last night's hotel in Nizwa.

The plan next day was to drive to Sur, on the coast, via an area called Wahabi Sands. This was sand dune country, inhabited by Bedouin, where you could drive into the desert. That amounted to following a track down a broad, sandy valley flanked by dunes and punctuated by occasional small Bedouin encampments. The track was loose, but not hard for a 4wd.

Ranging off to the left and right was easier than it looked because of a sort of crust on the sand. There were dead, dry bushes to avoid and sharp, spiky bits of roots sticking up. These areas were red, but there were also yellow sand hillocks. They had to be avoided because they had a sharp drop-off on the lee side and were quite dangerous.

The dunes themselves we did not attempt, partly because it was a hire car, partly because it was too much trouble to let down the tyres just to mess about, but mostly because I wouldn't have been game anyway. Overall, the experience was interesting enough without deliberately getting silly and frightening Sheri in the process.

It was a hot, windy day. Later, back on the highway at a steady 130, we saw several dust spouts whirling. We stopped for a while at a river valley with clear, green water, quite appealing.

Around four p.m. we got to Sur, a coastal town. There was a large sea inlet. On one side of this, tidal flats were a haven for large fishing dhows. Several derelict boats lay bleaching their bones in the sun. A boat yard stood beyond, where a new dhow was being built. The tools were modern, but the design was traditional.

Not far away was a restored vessel, seventy years old, a beautiful, classic dhow. It had been brought back from Yemen where it had spent its working life and had been put on display in permanent dry dock. I paced it out at thirty five metres long.

A small aluminium boat, what in Australia would be called a "tinny", ferried us across the narrow neck of the lagoon. On the other side was a large headland. Many houses were built on it, a coastal get-away for Omanis. Sur proper was on the other side of the inlet.

Feral goats fossicked amongst the rubbish bins and trotted between the houses. Of course there were no fences and few roads—you just picked your way. One goat was capering about on a car bonnet. Better than stray dogs, I thought. Perhaps Omanis liked to be reminded of their desert heritage—the goats had no other function that I could see.

A bit of navigational bumbling caused us to pass the big new LNG gasworks by the coast. A long conveyer belt jutted out into the sea, while on the horizon a huge gas bulk carrier lay anchored. There was clearly a lot of money in Oman and this was one of the reasons.

We found our way to the right road, running between the rugged mountains and the coast. We weren't amazed to see a new dual highway under construction, along which we were directed by the foreman of a Japanese construction team. As usual in Oman, things weren't being done by halves. This huge new road was being built by many teams, all Japanese, over a very long distance. It included great bridges, soaring over wadis.

Soon we were led onto a rough side road, which gave way to the original, very rough coastal road. This was part of the reason we had the 4wd—the guide book had warned us that nothing less would do. Very little traffic used it. Yet the new road would be a magnificent highway: the Omanis were taking the long view.

About fifty kilometres from Sur we passed through a tiny town called Tiwi. The road through was a winding street, so narrow that in places you could not have passed a large vehicle. We didn't meet one, though.

Just beyond the town the little rough road plunged so steeply down to the sea I thought we must have missed our way. I pulled over and Sheri got out to check on foot before we committed ourselves to the sharp descent with an apparent full stop at the bottom. As she did so, a little flock of goats gathered at the top of a seven metre drop, only to be driven over it by a shepherd boy. The goats scampered down the seemingly-vertical cliff, clearly immune from gravity.

The road did turn at the bottom, so down we went. After only a kilometre or two, we came to Wadi Sham. This, we knew, would provide a really good walk, so we pulled in and took the camera and our swimming costumes.

The wadi climbed gradually up between towering mountains, punctuated by clear, greenish pools. There was just enough flat land for palm trees and gardens, but not houses. In any case it looked like too much water would come down in the Khareef, the monsoon. We could see old, stone water channels, but now water pipes had largely replaced them.

One unprepossessing fellow tried to chat us up—he wanted to be our guide. We refused, but he followed about thirty metres behind. We stopped. He stopped. I approached him and said we didn't want a guide. He argued. I said he could walk where he wanted, it was his village, but we wanted to walk alone. He argued again. I made it abundantly clear that we wanted no part of his company and walked away from him. Slowly he wandered ahead, while we delayed.

The pools got bigger and deeper as we went upstream, and now the water was running. Eventually we reached a point where we could go no further. Two westerners and a local man were already there, down by a deep pool, obviously about to swim. Spladoosh! Someone jumped in from about five metres up. It was our unwelcome friend from earlier: he'd teamed up with a mate.

They swam off upstream and we changed our clothes. Sheri wore a wrapper around her costume for the sake of local notions of modesty. The water was cool and felt good—the day was hot now.

Another couple and local guide arrived. The woman changed and swam, but the man sat clothed on a rock until the woman urged him to swim. English reticence I thought, judging from his accent.

After an hour's walk back to the Prado, we left. There were some difficult bits of road to negotiate as well as lots of rocky stretches, but the car ate it up. We passed through a place called Quryiat. After that the road was good bitumen for the remaining seventy five kilometres to Muscat.

We filled up with petrol, ready to hand back the vehicle. In three days we'd done one thousand kilometres and averaged twelve litres per hundred kilometres. Pretty good, I thought. The petrol was really cheap, about forty five cents per litre.

This was our last day in Oman. We found a better hotel than the dubious El Fanar, or 'Fanny Hotel' as Sheri liked to call it. In the souk she finally bought five of the mosque alarm clocks she wanted as gifts for friends. I had always teased her about them. They were neon pink or green plastic mosques that woke you to a recorded muezzin's call, and, to my mind, were the last word in kitsch.

"I tell you," she said as I was writing my journal, "Once the news is out, they'll be fighting over them back in Australia. I'll be hard put to keep one for myself."

" I just wrote that down."

"Arsehole!"

Off to the airport next morning, where I bought a nifty little lightweight plastic bottle of whiskey. An Indian man at the checkout had three litres of cheap whiskey. But Sheri was behind another man, also Indian, who bought twenty litres. Even the checkout operator was surprised!

SHARJAH AND DUBAI

It was only a short flight out of Oman into Sharjah, back in the United Arab Emirates. We took an airport taxi driven by a woman wearing a shawl rather than the full burqua, a first for us. The hotel was the very decent place we'd stayed in when we were starting out.

Sheri contacted the expats from Dubai that we'd met in Salalah and who'd invited us to stay with them. So that was arranged for tomorrow.

It was a lazy day for me after that. Sheri went souvenir and gift hunting while I watched a film and read books in the hotel. Later we went out together, finishing with an excellent meal in an Indian vegetarian restaurant. It appeared the whole district was Indian—there was hardly an Arab to be seen.

It seemed to me there was prejudice against these people, nearly all Tamil men. We'd read in the paper that Arab employers sometimes ignored contracts and refused to bring out an Indian worker's family. So the worker might be away from his family for years, his only option being to break his contract and go home. Of course there would be penalties …

Then too, in the airport that morning, a well-dressed young Indian man had set off the metal detector when he walked through. This would normally result in being patted down—it had happened to me many times on this trip. But he this man was rudely told to take off his shoes. Again he set off the beeper. Now he was abruptly told to take off his belt. This time he got through.

It seemed to me a humiliating procedure. I supposed there was a whole lot more to know about Indian-Omani relations, but little things can say a lot. The same airport official who was so abrupt to the Indian was very polite to me, a Westerner in late middle age.

In the night the air-con stopped working and I woke to a still, hot room. So I put on a shirt over my pajama shorts and took the lift down ten floors to tell the night manager. Then I went back up.

Soon a man came to the hotel door. Sheri was still sleeping inside and I beckoned him inside, putting a finger to my lips at the same time. No wonder he hesitated! However, he entered and simply pressed a re-set button, after which we had no problems.

In the morning we slept in a bit, and just before twelve took a taxi to our acquaintances in Dubai.

Ron and Chris had an apartment near the centre. They gave us lunch, after which we all got into their 4wd for a look around. Ron was a senior design engineer and responsible for one of the city's major developments, a multi-fingered artificial island that would house a great many people. Dubai was a paradise for him; he revelled in the innovative designs of the big buildings, pointing them out as we travelled.

Hundreds of new apartment buildings were going up at a phenomenal rate. According to an Australian TV program that coincidentally showed that evening, Dubai was the fastest-growing city in the world: only one and a half million currently, but aiming for five million in the next several years. Unbelievable, yet we'd seen the evidence. And virtually all of these would be foreigners. The local population was only a quarter of a million.

We visited a beach where many Western women wore bikinis, a novel sight in this Moslem environment. After that came a vast shopping centre, elaborately decorated in themes suiting different countries. There were restaurants, coffee shops and an extensive waterway with boats for hire. It was where people went for a good time on their days off.

All of this had been achieved by an army of half a million cheap labourers and tradesmen from Pakistan and India. They worked for very small wages and lived in very poor accommodation. Last year eight hundred of them had died in construction accidents.

Ron and Chris also showed us huge, palatial houses on private estates of many acres. These belonged to the sons and daughters of the ruling families. One was jet black, a private joke by one known as the "Black Prince". The affluence of Dubai was incredible. Our earlier three-day stopover had not revealed that. It took local insight to show us.

Ron and Chris came from the little town of Picton on the South Island of New Zealand. They had a yacht there which they used to cruise the Pacific. But their plan when they left Dubai was to buy a boat locally or in Europe and spend the next five or six years sailing. They seemed to be the sort of people who were very capable of achieving their dreams, something not given to everyone.

A quiet day followed. Sheri and I went to the Dubai Creek area, where she spent most of her time pottering about in shops while I sat in a riverside coffee shop and read newspapers. Around four p.m. we took a slow taxi back through traffic-jammed roads to Ron and Chris's place. We sat and chatted for and hour or so, finished packing and caught a cab for the airport.

We were early for the check-in and read books while we waited. Suddenly the muezzin's call to prayer came over the PA system. We'd never had that happen in an airport before.

"Time to get out of here," I said.

And it was. We'd had a good time, an interesting time, and seen a lot in six weeks. But now we were ready to go, though a week in Thailand would be a good staging-post. If we were lucky we'd sleep on the plane overnight.

THAILAND

Not much sleep on the plane after all. We chose seats at the back of the plane, knowing that often whole rows of seats might be left vacant. But there was almost a full complement and, down at the back, the passengers were a fairly motley lot, to put it mildly. We did manage to get one empty seat beside us, so Sheri curled up across two seats with her feet on me. I did the manly thing and endured.

By 8.30 a.m. we were disembarking, having set our watches forward three hours. The New Siam 2 was already booked, so that was no problem. The room was good, the travellers here were a laid-back lot, and the young women behind the counter were sweeties. Bangkok was a relaxing place to come back to.

Sheri showered and soon dropped off to sleep. After a while, so did I.

Around 4 p.m. we woke up. I went down to see a travel agent who had an office in the foyer. However, she spoke poor English and wouldn't even give me a photocopy of their day-tour program to show Sheri, no doubt in case I tried to compare prices with other agents. So we wouldn't be dealing with them!

There was a swimming pool right next to the hotel restaurant. Sheri came down and we swam and read for a couple of hours, a nice, luxurious feeling.

Already Bangkok had absorbed us. We had stepped from one existence to another. The Arab world had closed behind us, but now the Thai world opened up.

In the cool of the evening we went out into the casual, colourful swirl of restaurants, open-air bars, shops, stalls, travel agents, tuk-tuks, women selling this and that, and men doing the same. There were travellers of all ages and states of dress—the whole lively sprawl of Banglamphu. We couldn't escape the curious mix of sights and smells, of decay and fertility, of youth and age, wealth and poverty, beauty and ugliness—all ingredients of the close, humid atmosphere of Bangkok. Nor did we want to. We would make day-trips to other places, but our base would be right here.

After breakfast it began to rain. Heavier and heavier it fell, for over an hour. When eventually we went out I had to carry my sandals to wade through puddles. Sheri wore rubber thongs, a better idea.

I sold a couple of novels to a second-hand bookshop. Then, at a little tour office, we booked a day trip up to Ayutthaya.

Over lunch I had a stubby of beer. Maybe that's what caused me to enter into a kind of deep awareness of the scene around me. Even the drips of water from an overhead drainpipe were intensely absorbing. This cheap stone didn't last long, broken by a conversation, but Bangkok does lend itself to that sort of thing. Other than that, it was a quiet day of walking along the river and reading. We weren't here for a hard time.

In the morning someone came to get us at the hotel. We walked around to the tour office where a few people were already waiting. Twenty minutes later, the little group was led off to a small bus, which stopped at a number of hotels to pick up other people.

Eventually we were off. In the bus, and later as we walked around, the guide indulged in long, boring information sessions. His English was really bad, his accent terrible. Frequently he punctuated his sentences with “Ya!”, as if to reassure himself that everything was understood.

Ayuthaya is a sizeable town about eighty kilometres north of Bangkok. There are many old temples scattered through it. However, it seemed tedious stuff to us, spoilt by some of the best ancient sites in the world. Old wats, built of flat bricks, had lost their covering of mortar. Enormous reclining Buddhas were impressive, but showed little variation. The buildings, what remained of them, had not the wonderful precision of the temples in Petra, for example. Nor were there any statues in good repair, except those reposing Buddhas. Even they were a bit of a cop-out from my point of view because they looked so easy to construct, as against standing ones.

The heat was building. By late afternoon it was 39 humid degrees. The little tour bus took us from place to place. People dispersed, looked around and returned to a rendezvous point.

At one stage Sheri was late back at a meeting point. We each had mobiles so I tried to phone her. After a moment I got a call. But it was my cousin Sylvia from Perth, last seen around thirty years ago! It turned out she was visiting Adelaide and had thought to surprise me. She did. But she was even more surprised to find the person on the other end of the phone was somewhere in the middle of Thailand, rather than in Adelaide.

Late in the afternoon we saw the king's palace. There were lots of lakes, a large neo-classical building, and beautiful furniture. You could hire a golf buggy if you didn't want to walk. Then we climbed a very tall tower, a sweaty exercise in this climate.

There was a thermometer on the bus heading back which showed the outside temperature. It fell steadily as we neared Bangkok in the evening, showing 29 degrees as we pulled in. The bus stopped somewhere around Banglapmphu and the guide jumped off.

"Happy New Year!" he called. (the Songkram festival was very near) Then he was gone.

Everyone got off. Sheri and I found our way back through a narrow alley lined with lit-up stalls. It was good to get back to the hotel, shower off the day's sweat and change into fresh clothes.

The evening was very warm. Khaosan Road was nearby, but was a different scene from where we staying, behind the wat. Khaosan was brassy, bustling, noisy and raw. Scantily-clad Thai girls were enticing people into various venues. Bright lights illuminated hundreds of fluttering red Coca-Cola flags strung across the street. Music blasted from places selling copies of CD's and film DVD's. Yet most of the people on the street were ordinary travellers, mostly young, but quite a few older people too. Not many would be buying sex— this was not the red light district. Plenty of the younger crowd seemed drunk, however.

It was too hot and noisy to eat here. We went back to our usual area, found a cool spot at an outside restaurant and had a good meal. Later we watched "Million Dollar Baby" in our hotel room.

Next day we went to Jim Thompson's house in Bangkok. This collection of six teak houses, bought separately from different parts of the country, was blended into one little estate set in beautiful gardens by an American who re-established Thai silk printing in the 1950's. He was a creative person with a lot of style—even today the place is very appealing. He disappeared without trace on a visit to the Cameron Highlands in Malaysia, aged sixty-one. It was somehow moving to look on what a man had done and know that he not grown old with it, nor moved on to something else, but simply vanished.

Later we walked through some of the busiest streets of the city, with the old centre of the road taken up by a three-storey overhead concrete structure. The lowest level was for pedestrians. We guessed one level was for the sky train, the other for motor vehicles. It towered above, blocking out much of the sky. The result was ear-shattering traffic noise blaring all around us, both from our own street level and from above.

Then the wind blew up, whirling dust into our eyes. It was horrible and we took refuge in a huge, ultra-modern, department-store building called "Central World." Here Sheri scouted the shops while I browsed in a book shop. We had lunch, paying by an electronic billing card that was new to us.

A side exit led us to a ferry route. We clambered onto a long, narrow boat with a roof and plastic spray sheets along the sides. This roared along at twenty knots or so, rocking violently as it hit the wash from another ferry. The klong was narrow, the motion of the boat violent, and spray was thrown high. Sheri thought it great fun, except for trying to climb over the high guard-wire of the boat in her skirt when we got on.

The ferry reached a terminal point, so we flagged down a tuk-tuk. He wanted one hundred baht. I offered twenty. When he poo-pood that I said: "OK, we get somebody else," a response which was never a bluff on my part and usually got results. We settled on forty.

Back at Banglamphu we booked a tour for the next day. In the process a Songkram procession passed by, playing music and showing banners held by some very beautiful girls.

Again, next day, we were out before seven. Nine of us, mostly young people, gathered for a mini-bus. It was a two and a half hour journey to the cemetery at Kanchanaburi, where seven thousand allied soldiers lay, victims of Death Railway.

It was a clear, open place. All the headstones were the same, apart from the inscriptions. They represented only a small proportion of all who died.

Not far away was the notorious Bridge on the River Kwai, although it was not the original. It spanned the muddy, swirling water. Nearby was an old museum which contained some deeply-moving exhibits.

One was a group of fairly crude but life-size figures, tall and thin, of emaciated POW's. They were lying in shallow water, almost naked, riddled with bloody wounds. The plaque said that the first bridge built (a wooden one, as in the film) had been under attack by allied aircraft. The Japanese had forced many men to stand on the bridge and wave, in an attempt to ward off the planes. Instead they had been bombed and the bridge was destroyed. The name of the American pilot was given.

We were led to a bamboo raft with several rows of benches. As people filled them, the raft settled lower until the floor was almost submerged. Cockroach-like insects scuttled out. The Thai boatman passed out some paddles and stood at the front of the raft, keeping one for himself. But he gave no directions to the paddlers, so it was a bit of a kerfuffle.

We pushed out into the current and steered an erratic path down the river, mostly traveling at an angle instead of pointing straight. We were almost pinned against one of the broad, concrete bridge supports. Then, as we finally approached the landing, the raft would not move through the water-weed that blocked our path. I picked up a long bamboo pole and shoved us in.

Lunch was on a floating restaurant, very scenic. We'd already been transferred to bench seats in the back of a covered utility and now we drove for perhaps forty-five minutes to something called the Tiger Temple. Set up by a monk, it was a rescue centre for tigers. The grounds were large and contained a variety of animals and birds, but the focal point was a little canyon. At the bottom were six or seven tigers on short chains.

There were many handlers. Almost all the tigers were lolling about;—they could have been sedated. A handler, male or female, would take a visitor by the arm and escort him or her to a tiger. So they did to me and, separately, to Sheri.

There was already a female tourist sitting with her head on the flank of the first tiger. Suddenly another beast roared from behind. The first tiger half-started up, giving the woman a good scare. Sedated it may have been, but totally harmless? Definitely not!

It was quite good fun, but I didn't find it very scary, figuring that it wouldn't be happening if it were dangerous. Still, the handler gripped my arm firmly. When I made a joke to the woman who'd been alarmed, the handler didn't like it. Too noisy? Maybe the wrong attitude as well!

I was led from tiger to tiger and encouraged to caress them, while another handler used our camera to take pictures. I didn't put my head on any flanks, though.

The monk who headed this project sat nearby with an air of gentle benevolence. The handlers were not monks, just young people who were probably quite dedicated to their work.

Sheri and I wandered around the rest of the grounds. In one place a group of semi-wild boar piglets skittered about. They were lean, with mottled fur. Sheri was able to entice the boldest one to come near for some food, prompting a monk to call down to us from a two-story building. He seemed a good-natured and friendly man.

Next was another vehicle trip and a ride on a rickety old train along Death Railway. The area was still rural, like most of Thailand.

Some of the rail cuttings led high above the river. I stood on the lower step of the connecting platform between the carriages to give Sheri a good view over my head. It was scary enough to spice up a great view, and I thought of the men who'd slaved and suffered, driving these rugged cuttings through.

The train clattered along, carrying some locals and a group of elderly Germans. When we got off we were driven to the little, rustic restaurant where we'd had lunch.

It was the end of the day and we had to wait for another van to take us back to Bangkok. Rain fell gently, which suited the scruffy, tropical environment. We stayed in the bigger part of the place, built on land instead of over the water. A few locals played pool, not very well. Sheri got a couple of coffees, an achievement in these parts.

I walked through the rain across the walkway to the empty, floating restaurant and looked back to the shore. Rain stippled the river and dripped from every roof, whether rough thatch or rusty iron. Bushy vegetation hung heavy with water. A canoe tied to the pontoon was half full. It was one of those achingly-perfect scenes that are pure gold to a traveller.

It was dark before we were back in the van with the original morning's group. It had been broken up through the day because there had been different things to choose from. This had resulted in delays for some, waiting for another vehicle to collect them. One couple was very annoyed, especially the man. He looked like The World's Most Laid-Back Hippy, but he was complaining bitterly and insisting on a refund. Good luck with that, we thought. If you can't go with the flow in Thailand you'll probably get spat out!

It was around 8.30 in the evening when we got back to Banglamphu. Songkram was in full swing. People were having a riotous time with high-powered water pistols and a kind of white paste, a sort of fertility blessing. We had to run a long gauntlet through jets of water, some ice-cold, though we didn't get paste-smeared. It was good to get back, shower and have dinner. It had been a long day.

Sheri was sound asleep when I woke, so I went down to breakfast with a book. Later we set out, but rain began to fall. There were still groups of people, mostly children, with water guns. We retreated to the hotel. But by midday the sky had cleared and we went to the local ferry stop, Pra A-Thit. I wanted to take Sheri on a klong boat trip in a more scenic part of the city than our first ride seven weeks ago.

The ticket seller wanted silly money, a thousand baht each, but when I began to leave she asked me what I'd pay. Five hundred baht for both, I replied. She accepted. But soon after that a problem arose because she thought she'd already given me five hundred baht change from my thousand note. I insisted, even showing my wallet and empty pockets. Reluctantly she gave me the five hundred, but seemed unconvinced.

It was just Sheri and me on the long-tail, those sleek, graceful boats with a bellowing motor-car engine mounted on a pivot, with a long tube projecting behind and a thrashing propellor at the end. The Chao Phraya was choppy from the wind, but even allowing for that we made slow progress. The driver was on his mobile phone and kept backing the throttle to an idle so he could have a conversation. He kept this up even in the quiet waters of the klong until I gestured for him to get a move on.

Other boats came towards us, passing fairly close. One middle-aged Westerner looked straight at me as he passed and, without a trace of a smile, squirted me in the face. "Arsehole!" I thought, but said nothing. Songkram was Songkram. Quite a few children and adults squirted us from stilt-houses, but that was all good-natured.

We cruised past temples and schools as well as houses. Here, the klong was about fifty metres wide. Once Bangkok had largely consisted of these waterways, before the sprawl.

Sometimes people bathed or swam at the edges, something I wouldn't have wanted to do. The boatman seemed to know one man who was washing himself waist-deep in front of his house, so stopped for a chat.

The trip in the long-prowed boat took over an hour and we enjoyed it. Back on the main river we banged and slammed over the choppy little waves, catching brownish spray on our faces. At the wharf the ticket-seller had counted her money and found it correct, so she was all smiles. I hadn't had the feeling she was anything but genuine and this confirmed it.

We took the main ferry to Chinatown. These boats were big, fast and cheap—the river made a good highway. Many places in Chinatown were shut for the festival, but there was enough to be interesting. We had a rice and duck lunch in a restaurant with a very low ceiling but plenty of customers, copped a few squirts on the way back to the hotel, then spent a quiet afternoon lounging in the hotel room.

In the morning Sheri thought the water-squirting had probably stopped and suggested we go off to sell a few books we had finished. However, the shops were shut and the water enthusiasts were still keen. So we took a ferry to a big complex called Riverside which sold all kinds of artworks.

On the ground floor was a display of paintings, many of them portraits of the king. He appeared to be a fairly unprepossessing man of average size, unequal eye height, messy hair and, always, an oversized pair of spectacles.

The whole place seemed to be full of expensive objects that had no buyers. We had a coffee and, later, lunch at a second-floor restaurant with good views of the river. Then, having seen what there was to see, we returned to the hotel and took it easy.

This was the end of our wind-down week. We ate at the same restaurant as last night, partly because it was relatively safe from passing water-pistol patrols. The young travellers had tired of the fun, but plenty of young Thais were still up for it. Unlike the foreigners they didn't squirt restaurant patrons and they weren't drunk. They just livened the place up.

Dinner took an hour to arrive, but we already knew we could expect that. We weren't in a hurry. Even so, by 9.45 we were back home.

Knowing we had an all-night flight in front of us, we slept well and rose late. I took a last walk to see if I could get rid of those unwanted books. The lane was dry, which told me that the water-throwers were finally taking a rest. The bookshops were open but, having been shut for days and taken no money, were not inclined to buy anything. So we left them for the hotel to give away.

This final walk reminded me of how much I liked this little part of Bangkok. Such a happening place in its own quiet way, except during Songkram when it became an enjoyably noisy place.

We had a late check-out and sat in the foyer with our bags, reading the morning papers. There I saw that a group of Thai holiday-makers had been drowned in a flash-flood in a southern province. Villagers had seen the water turning muddy and warned them, but many had paid no attention.

A taxi collected us at 1.30 and soon we were doing 140 kph on the toll-way, passing everyone.

"Take it easy. There's no hurry," I said, but he only sped up to 150. No tip for him!

The usual way of passing time in an airport includes buying duty-free shopping, of course. This time we met with a problem. When Sheri took some bottles of cosmetics to the check-out, the attendant asked where we were going.

"Australia", Sheri answered.

"So sorry, you cannot take any liquids on the plane. New regulations this week."

Bloody anti-terrorist measures! But only for Australia, apparently. Typical. Watch out for that perfume, it might blow up.

At the gate entrance was a long queue. Everyone had to empty their cabin baggage out for inspection. All sorts of liquid containers were dumped in a large box. It was a slow, tedious and ineffably stupid process. I wondered whose outstandingly bright idea it had been …

Neither of us slept for more than half an hour on the plane. Through an uncurtained window I watched the Australian sun creep up over the vast, curved horizon, the red glow stealing all along, a paler blue above fading into deep night blue, across the endless land. A great sight, one I always love.

Sydney looked wonderful in the early morning as the plane droned towards the airport, all waterways and well-greened city. We bought duty-free whiskey and transferred to a flight for Adelaide. It wasn't quite that simply, however. Australian security is at once more relaxed and chatty than other countries and yet much more fussy. So I had to go back and forth through the metal detector, taking off this or that, but still setting the damned thing off. Finally I said: "Just pat me down." But there was no-one to do it—the female official couldn't, and she was alone.

Underslept and irritable, I called out to the next checking aisle, which had two officials, "Is there a patter there?" My patience was very thin. Eventually the fellow interrupted his chat long enough to come and pat me down.

After that we waited in a long line to get through customs, another first for the trip. When it was our turn they only x-rayed our baggage although other people were thoroughly checked, but we didn't complain about that.

At last we boarded our plane and around 11.30 we landed in Adelaide. It was a clear, bright day in the low twenties. We were home, and glad of it. I think that's just how things should be, don't you?

www.ingramcontent.com/pod-product-compliance
Ingram Content Group UK Ltd.
Pitfield, Milton Keynes, MK11 3LW, UK
UKHW020240250726
13967UKWH00001B/475

9 781447 726289